P9-AQX-433

OVERVIEW
OF THE
PSYCHOTHERAPIES

Overview of the Psychotherapies

Edited by

GENE USDIN, M.D.

Clinical Professor of Psychiatry
Louisiana State University School of Medicine

Introduction by Melvin Sabshin, M.D.

BRUNNER/MAZEL, *Publishers* • NEW YORK

Copyright © 1975 by The American College of Psychiatrists
Published by
BRUNNER/MAZEL, INC.
64 University Place, New York, N. Y. 10003

Library of Congress Cataloging in Publication Data
Main entry under title:

OVERVIEW OF THE PSYCHOTHERAPIES.

Outgrowth of the 1974 conference of the American College of
Psychiatrists.
Includes bibliographies.
1. Psychotherapy—Congresses. I. Usdin, Gene L., ed. II. American
College of Psychiatrists.
[DNLM: 1. Psychotherapy—Congresses. VM420 096 1974]
RC480.092 1975   616.8'914   74-84149
ISBN 0-87630-099-9

MANUFACTURED IN THE UNITED STATES OF AMERICA

AMERICAN COLLEGE OF PSYCHIATRISTS

Officers

Melvin Sabshin, M.D., *President*

Hamilton Ford, M. D.
President-Elect
Hayden H. Donahue, M.D.
First Vice-President
Peter A. Martin, M. D.
Second Vice-President

John C. Nemiah, M.D.
Secretary-General
Charles E. Smith, M.D.
Treasurer
John D. Trawick, Jr. M.D.
Archivist-Historian

Program Committee for 1974 Annual Meeting

Gene Usdin, M.D. *Chairman*

Norman Q. Brill, M.D.
Robert W. Gibson, M.D.
Burton J. Goldstein, M.D.
Donald C. Greaves, M.D.

Harold Hiatt, M.D.
Hyman L. Muslin, M.D.
S. Mouchly Small, M.D.
Robert L. Williams, M.D.

Publications Committee

Gene Usdin, M.D. *Chairman*
Charles K. Hofling, M.D., *Vice-Chairman*

Francis J. Braceland, M.D.
D. Earl Brown, Jr., M.D.
Paul Jay Fink, M.D.
Henry P. Laughlin, M.D.

John C. Nemiah, M.D.
Harold Visotsky, M.D.
Warren Williams, M.D.

CONTRIBUTORS

ANN BRINKLEY-BIRK, Ph.D.,
   Research Director, Learning Therapies, Inc., Newton, Mass.

LEE BIRK, M.D.
   Clinical Director, Learning Therapies, Inc., Newton, Mass.; Assistant Clinical Professor of Psychiatry, Harvard Medical School

JEROME D. FRANK, M.D.
   Professor of Psychiatry, The Henry Phipps Psychiatric Clinic, The Johns Hopkins University School of Medicine

SHERVERT H. FRAZIER, M.D.
   Psychiatrist-in-Chief, McLean Hospital, Belmont, Mass.; Professor of Psychiatry, Harvard University Medical School

MORTON A. LIEBERMAN, Ph.D.
   Professor, Department of Behavioral Sciences (Human Development) and Department of Psychiatry, University of Chicago

PETER A. MARTIN, M.D.
Clinical Professor of Psychiatry at Wayne State University School of Medicine and the University of Michigan School of Medicine

HYMAN L. MUSLIN, M.D.
Professor and Acting Head, Department of Psychiatry, The Abraham Lincoln School of Medicine, University of Illinois at the Medical Center

JOHN C. NEMIAH, M.D.
Professor of Psychiatry, Harvard University Medical School; Psychiatrist-in-Chief, Beth Israel Hospital, Boston, Mass.

MELVIN SABSHIN, M.D.
Medical Director, American Psychiatric Association

GEORGE SASLOW, M.D.
Chief, Mental Health and Behavioral Sciences Section, Veterans Administration Hospital, Sepulveda, Cal.

JOSEPH ZUBIN, Ph.D.
Chief of Psychiatric Research, Biometrics Research, State of New York Department of Mental Hygiene

CONTENTS

ix

PART III: THE STANLEY R. DEAN
AWARD LECTURE

Foreword

Founded in 1963, The American College of Psychiatrists is a professional organization whose primary purpose is to develop a program of postgraduate education for its members and fellows. From an initial membership of 30, the College has grown over the past decade to nearly 500. Among its membership are many of the leaders of North American psychiatry, and admission to the organization has become a mark of recognition and honor for those who are invited to join.

A number of committees that meet regularly during the year, as well as the semi-annual meeting of the officers and the Board of Regents, enable the College to carry on its organizational business as a background to the Annual Meeting for all members. It is here that a carefully planned scientific program is presented for the education of the membership. Each meeting is devoted to a single theme of importance to psychiatrists, and the format consists of lectures given by selected speakers, followed by extensive small group discussions.

Of central importance to the educational program are the activities of the Continuing Education Committee, which maintains an ongoing study of the uses and problems of postgraduate education. With an eye to being in the vanguard of postgraduate education, the College has been innovative in its meeting formats. For the annual meeting of 1974, from which this volume derives, a videotape of an evaluation interview was prepared by a College member and this videotape was circulated to the program participants. Then, following a presentation of "An Overview of Psychotherapy," the videotape was shown to all registrants at the meeting. Following this, distinguished authorities of various types of psychotherapy related to the videotape and then discussed their particular school of therapy. After each plenary session, the College members broke up into small groups for discussions. At the conclusion of the meeting, a self-assessment examination, based on questions supplied by the meeting lecturers, was given.

Not the least of the College's educational efforts are its publications, which derive from the Annual Meetings and have had a wide readership. Starting with the first publication in 1969 on the subject of psychoanalysis in present-day psychiatry, and continuing with volumes on psychiatry and anthropology, violence, sleep research, and education and image of psychiatrists, these volumes have addressed themselves to a broad range of topics. They are unified, however, not only by the light they throw on areas that are of continuing significance in psychiatric theory, research, and clinical practice, but by their concern with the future development and thrust of psychiatry as one of the most basic disciplines contributing to an understanding of man and an enhancement of the human condition.

GENE USDIN, M.D.

Introduction

Melvin Sabshin, M.D.

Each conference on psychotherapy tends to have a distinctive character and style depending upon the varying perspectives, abilities and inclinations of those who plan the program. The clinical pragmatist prefers to focus his attention upon how to treat patient A who suffers from condition X; a more abstract theorist might be inclined towards a conference that includes discussion of where psychotherapy fits into a larger social context of force-fields affecting basic human values and hence human problems in coping. Implicit as well as explicit definitions of psychotherapy determine whether or not such subjects as behavioral modification or psychopharmacology are included in a psychotherapy conference. Some program planners are especially earnest in seeking to present a wide variety of psychotherapeutic approaches; others limit the range to a few prototype examples. Those with research interests will be more likely to include process or outcome data and they will focus upon particular methodological issues. All of these variables are compounded by sub-themes and branching into multiple alternatives. For example, to what extent should actual clinical interaction (e.g., videotapes) be presented and in what depth should they be discussed? The ultimate shape of the conference depends heavily on how the planners orchestrate these themes and whom they select to play the instruments.

The conference which culminated in this volume was designed to serve a continuing education function for the membership of the American College of Psychiatrists and that purpose necessarily dominated the proceedings. The College itself has matured into a significant educational vehicle and the 1974 meeting was a prototype of high-level learning. It is important to note that those in attendance were exceptionally well-motivated students who responded actively in the sessions and participated fully in an experimental instrument designed to evaluate their competence in understanding the subjects covered during the seminar.

Jerome Frank's overview provides the historical and the current contextual framework for this monograph. Even highly sophisticated readers will want to re-read this paper several times when they begin to understand the profoundness of the questions and when they ponder the various implications. On superficial examination of recent trends, the proliferating newer schools of psychotherapy appear to reflect a chaotic flowering of multiple approaches. As Frank plunges into this thicket, he attempts to demonstrate how "psychotherapy can be viewed as a social institution created to fill the gap left by the decay of other institutions which gave meaning to life and a feeling of connectedness to others." In addition to documenting force fields affecting psychotherapy as whole, Frank also discusses how these forces affect therapists as well as patients. Building from this base, he attempts to synthesize the features common to or shared by all psychotherapies.

Frank's paper also includes remarks pertinent to diagnosis and classification; Frank stresses his hope that "it might be more profitable to classify patients with respect to their relative predilection for or ability to respond to therapies which emphasize one of the shared features above another." Not surprisingly, Frank emphasizes pluralism in the education of the mental health professional so that the trainee can make a rational choice to concentrate on an approach "congenial to his own personality." Very few psychiatrists have the vision to be able to see how the implicit values of psychotherapy have such a profound impact on our practice. Frank makes the point with grace and parsimony when he states that the psychotherapeutic literature contains "precious little on the redemptive power of suffering, acceptance of one's lot in life, filial piety, adherence to tradition, self-restraint and moderation." Perhaps some day in the not-too-distant future, colleagues from other countries with differing values concerning these variables will make that point even more vividly as the field of transcultural comparison of psychotherapy begins to expand.

One of the most relevant aspects of "dynamic psychotherapy" for this monograph is the fact that it is now one of the "older" forms of therapy. The original controversies surrounding its inception have not been stilled, but the years have drained some of the intensity out of the debates, including the differences of opinion among psychoanalysts. It requires special talent to wade through the literature and to present a succinct as well as elegant summary of both classical psychoanalysis and dynamic psychotherapy. John Nemiah has, in fact, accomplished that difficult task and his paper is a clear overview. During his actual presentation the audience paid close attention and there were notable moments of assent in the audience when a half-familiar concept became familiar once more, or in many cases was clarified more precisely than ever before. The reader can utilize the paper in the same fashion, whether or not he or she has been educated extensively in the subject. For example, the discussion of "resistance" is particularly lucid, culminating in Nemiah's synthesizing comment that resistance is "the visible effect in the therapeutic situation of the very forces of repression and psychological conflict that had in the first place given rise to the compromise solution of symptoms that it was the aim of psychotherapy to remove."

In addition to the review of dynamic psychotherapy and psychoanalysis itself, Nemiah summarizes several recent developments in focused psychotherapy and anxiety-provoking psychotherapy. If, in fact, this type of treatment turns out to have the broad applicability predicted by the author, the implications for education and for practice are quite significant.

The last part of Nemiah's paper deals with his reaction to the videotaped clinical interview presented by Dr. Muslin. The discussion is illuminating since it helps the reader to understand more specifically how Nemiah's criteria for dynamic psychotherapy are actually applied. Furthermore, the author's willingness to utilize a "conservative regimen" of drugs and supportive therapies for the patient presented on the videotape demonstrates his own flexibility and pluralism.

Behavioral therapies are rather belatedly being employed by many psychiatrists and this volume is distinguished by the inclusion of two papers on this subject. Birk's discussion is especially pertinent since he builds a number of major conceptual bridges while making a consistent assault on stereotypes isolating one form of therapy from another. In contrast to some of his colleagues, Birk can move comfortably from behavioral therapies into the world of dynamic psychotherapy and tear down some of the walls between them in the process; "Insight serves to uncover the learned, developmental origins of maladaptive behavior, and behavioral change serves to highlight the increasingly conspicuous discrepancy between reality-based world and self assessment and a distorted, idiosyncratic cognitive set which, if unrealized, would continue to support both maladaptive behavior and negative world and self evaluation." In addition to combining behavioral and psychoanalytic principles, Birk makes a special point of emphasizing the natural social context in which the adaptive or maladaptive behavior is learned. It is this latter focus which makes the paper most outstanding for clinicians since the author translates the social contextual factors into significant therapeutic issues. The main body of the paper deals with group therapy, couple therapy, and direct sexual therapy. Birk discusses each of these approaches separately and then extracts common principles for all of them. In doing so, he emphasizes the value of direct observation in the relevant social context and helps the reader to integrate the use of behavioral therapy and insight-seeking approaches. For many psychiatrists who have been mildly phobic about reading the behavioral literature, this paper could very well serve as an effective change agent.

As was his charge from the Program Committee, Saslow focuses much more directly upon the specific videotaped case presented by Dr. Muslin. The learning value of his presentation is quite high since the contrasting styles and techniques between his approach and those of others are quite visible and clear. Furthermore, Saslow is a marvelous teacher with his enthusiasm, clarity of thought, and effective communication abilities. Like Birk, Saslow pays close attention to the situational context in which behavior occurs. In contrast to Birk, however, Saslow is more involved in demonstrating the behavioral methodology than in building bridges with other conceptual schema. The paper is replete with examples of encouragement of patients' strengths, the use of everyday language in communication with patients, the rationale for underemphasis of earlier patient-parent relationships, the use of daily logs and the choice of specific reinforcement techniques. The coupling of Birk's paper with that of Saslow is a particularly fortunate linkage. Many readers who are encouraged to delve more deeply into behavioral therapies by Birk's contextual comments will be motivated to explore the specifics embodied in Saslow's presentation. The opportunity to learn a great deal about the behavioral aspects of psychotherapy is significantly enhanced by the combination of the two papers.

Lieberman's overview of the group therapies is an excellent introduction for newcomers to the field. Simultaneously, however, it is a highly sophisticated, objective review of the critical issues facing those at the vanguard of group healing. In some ways these issues parallel the varying perspectives in the world of dyadic therapies, but Lieberman deplores the direct transfer of the intellectual battles from the dyadic to the group scene without examining their relevance to the groups.

One of the many nice touches in Lieberman's paper is the shift in level of discourse from theory to practice and back again to general principles and issues. For example, after discussing several of the "hot" conceptual conflicts in the group movement, he illustrates some of the issues by describing a typical initial session of a traditional group. It is obvious that he has been there and that he has the capacity to communicate what it is all about. Changing pace and style once again, he makes a lucid comparison among healing groups and then indicates the relationship of the newly developing growth centers and the human potential movement to the traditional mental health institutions. Lieberman's discussion of group leaders is particularly lucid and he helps the reader to integrate recent studies of these leaders to the issues underlying the very process of group healing. Like Birk, Lieberman is deeply involved in constructing bridges among various approaches and his paper fits in well with each of the other psychotherapeutic perspectives in this volume.

In my judgment, Dr. Usdin and his colleagues made a very wise decision in requesting a paper by Shervert Frazier on "Psychopharmacology in a Psychotherapeutic Setting." The absence of such a presentation in many symposia on psychotherapy isolates the discussion from the psychiatric mainstream. Indeed, Frazier's paper is in the heartland of psychiatric practice, reflecting the perspective of what most psychiatrists do or should do in the real world of the consulting room, the clinic, the hospital, and the community mental health center.

Like Saslow, Frazier devotes a good deal of attention to the evaluation and the management of the patient presented on the videotape. After outlining some of the information needed to prepare for an accurate use of psychopharmacological agents, he delineates his approach to crisis intervention and then outlines the rationale for specific pharmacotherapy. While precise in his discussion of this rationale, Frazier is clearly not a somatotherapeutic purist. Throughout his clinical discussion, he weaves the psychotherapeutic and the pharmacotherapeutic approaches together into an integrated balance. Unfortunately, Frazier's clarity in this matter is less common among mental health professionals than it should be, and one of psychiatry's major tasks involves helping the profession to understand the principles covered in this very fine presentation.

Peter Martin's superb clinical skills, warmth and conceptual clarity shine through his absorbing paper on "The Psychotherapy of Marital Partners: Old or New?" which was developed from a pre-meeting workshop which Martin conducted for College members. In addition, his level-headed pragmatism is evident in his efforts to help people achieve "a harmonious working marriage." One of the most innovative aspects of Martin's paper is his attempt to derive normal values for marriage by investigation of specific forms of psychopathology. After presentation of well-chosen clinical examples, he delineates a practical method of discerning the individual and the dyadic capacities and incapacities of marital pairs. The goal of the psychotherapy is to effect "a normalization of the pathological values" uncovered during the diagnostic evaluation.

The paper by Joseph Zubin on schizophrenia also did not arise directly out of the basic theme of the College meeting, but was the Stanley R. Dean Award presentation, given annually at the College meeting, on especially meritorious research pertinent to schizophrenia. The discussion of the vulnerabilities, predilections, and manifestations of schizophrenic patients is handled deftly and thoroughly by Zubin. Beyond that, however, Zubin enunciated a clear position on the role of biometrics in the evaluative processes. There is great need for analogous systems in approaching the more general problem of psychotherapeutic evaluation. For all of the research on this subject, it is clear that we are still at a primitive stage in clarifying the field of therapeutic outcome. Perhaps we are most lucid in evaluating therapeutic effectiveness of the most severe psychiatric disorders (e.g. bi-polar illness, certain forms of schizophrenia) when we employ reliable but gross measures of outcome. Our skills in evaluation are much less clear when talking about character disorders or conditions which reflect the psychopathology of everyday life. In this arena we continue to be beset by imprecision and conflicts regarding our basic concept of health as well as illness.

Taken together, the contributors to this symposium have presented a challenging overview of varied approaches to psychotherapy, exemplifying the use of psychoanalysis, behavioral modification, group therapy, pharmacotherapy, and marital therapy. The clear implication for the psychotherapist is that our therapeutic armamentarium will encompass a variety of approaches so that treatment can be geared to different patients and situations and not determined by a monolithic commitment to one therapeutic approach. The wide-ranging overview of theoretical and clinical viewpoints provided by this symposium makes this volume an invaluable addition to the thinking and practice of every therapist.

Part I
AN OVERVIEW

1

An Overview of Psychotherapy

Jerome D. Frank, M.D.

The prospect of preparing an overview of psychotherapy in
America today is enough to make the most stouthearted quail.
Gone are the days when the scene could be encompassed by
Freud, Jung and Adler, with side-glances at Rank, Horney and
Rogers. In the last two decades, psychotherapy has been undergoing a continuous explosion, and the end is not in sight. Its
targets have spread from individuals to families and groups,
and now whole neighborhoods. Methods range from traditional
interviews to tickling, nude marathons and elaborate rituals of
meditation; practitioners have broken the bounds of the traditional disciplines and now include many whose only training is
having undergone the therapy they offer to others, or who are
simply fellow sufferers. The settings in which therapy is conducted have burst out of hospitals and offices to living rooms,
motels and resorts, and new psychotherapies spring up almost
overnight.

This lush overgrowth, of course, is in response to public demand, which seems insatiable. Persons are not only flocking to
psychotherapies in droves, but are frantically searching for solutions to their personal problems in self-help books, which

3

repeatedly make bestseller lists. Two recent front runners were *I'm O.K., You're O.K.* (1) and *How To Be Your Own Best Friend* (2).

Actually, the situation may not be as chaotic as it appears. Much of the apparent confusion results from the understandable insistence by proponents of each therapy that their particular brand is uniquely different from its rivals. Similarly, although the consumers of psychotherapies seem superficially extremely diverse, the sources of distress for which they seek relief have much in common. All reflect disturbances in the person's communicative and symbolic functions, including his image of himself, of people close to him and, sometimes, of his place in the cosmos, as well as his social behavior. Underneath the diverse superficial manifestations of these disturbances, all candidates for psychotherapy suffer from dysphoric affects, particularly anxiety, depression, resentment and sense of alienation. Moreover, the patient and often those about him seek psychotherapy for him primarily because they despair of his being able to regain his emotional equilibrium and self-control without outside help. In short, I believe that persons seek psychotherapy chiefly because they are demoralized, and that the shared features of different psychotherapies, in which lie their main therapeutic efficacy, combat this state of mind (3, 4).

Furthermore, since the determinants of the patient's demoralization include early interactions with his family—the society's major agent of acculturation—as well as conflicts with the values and codes of conduct of his contemporaries, the patient's culture largely determines the nature of the stresses that have demoralized him and the ways in which he manifests this state of mind. Since psychotherapists are products of the same culture and derive their power and prestige from it, psychotherapeutic concepts and methods also are largely determined by features of the society that spawns them.

In this presentation, therefore, rather than attempting the

almost impossible tasks of making a systematic survey of the panoply of contemporary schools and methods of psychotherapy, I shall attempt to relate psychotherapy in a generic sense to forces in contemporary American society, consider the effects of these forces on both practitioners and patients, describe features shared by all forms of psychotherapy and, finally, very briefly consider some implications for classification of patients and training of therapists.

Let me approach the relationship of psychotherapy to society through an examination of some of the reasons for its extraordinary popularity and diversity in America today. In order to be psychologically comfortable, a person has to have confidence in his bodily health, feel that his life has significance and have confidence that he can love and be loved by others (5). Modern society has proved deficient in meeting these last two needs.

The triumphs of medical science have alleviated many forms of suffering and prolonged many lives, but have not changed the fact that there will always be 10 leading causes of death. To cope with this existential reality, humans have turned to religion for reassurance that their brief sojourn on earth has made a difference, if only to God. However, as a result of the challenges of scientific findings to many traditional religious beliefs, the power of traditional religions to give meaning to life has been seriously eroded. For a while it seemed as if the search for truth, as defined by science, might afford a sufficient substitute, especially in view of science's ability to bring so many betterments in the human lot. With the advent of nuclear weapons and the increasingly menacing pollution of the biosphere, however, science begins to look less like a savior and more like a Pied Piper leading mankind to destruction through the promise of endless goodies.

That psychotherapy can perform some of the same functions as religion is evidenced today by the blurring of the lines between psychotherapeutic schools and religious sects. Scientology, an outgrowth of Dianetics, has officially become a religion, and the messianic zeal of adherents to Transactional Analysis and Reevaluation Counseling, to mention only two, is indistinguishable from that of members of proselytizing religions. Furthermore, many currently flourishing religio-mystical cults, while not aimed at relieving specific symptoms, offer their acolytes the hope of achieving inner peace by the practice of rituals believed to enable them to escape from the tyranny of the individual ego and achieve union with the cosmic consciousness. Foreshadowed by Christian Science, such movements as Oscar Ichazo's Arica Institute, Maharishi Mahesh's Transcendental Meditation and the Divine Light Mission of Guru Maharaj ji are attracting thousands of suffering persons who in the past have turned to naturalistic forms of psychotherapy. While these religious movements share many features with schools of psychotherapy in the narrower sense, to keep this review from becoming impossibly complex I shall not consider them further.

The rush to psychotherapy has been stimulated not only by the decline of traditional religions but also by psychological insecurities resulting from unprecedentedly rapid changes in the conditions of life. This leads to questioning of traditional ethical values that offered guidelines for conduct. Consider, for example, what has happened to chastity and thrift in recent years. Since new values cannot achieve the acceptability and power of old, discredited ones until society has settled down, members of a changing society tend to lose their sense of direction.

The speed of social change has also disrupted the close, mutually supportive, enduring relationships so essential to our sense of well-being. It has especially undermined the ties of kinship, especially between generations, and substituted the shallow, self-serving affability of the housing development, the office and the club. Role relationships in which people use each other as objects are increasingly encroaching upon feeling relationships, which are sources of psychological support (6). As we seek to manipulate rather than care for each other, we have developed increasingly subtle techniques for concealing our intentions. Ruthlessness and deceptiveness are hidden behind masks of friendliness, warmth and sincerity. It becomes increasingly difficult to distinguish the liar from the honest man. So, in addition to being uncertain about why he is alive, modern man suffers from feelings of alienation and mistrust.

Finally, too many people today have too much money and not enough to do, and they turn to psychotherapy to combat the resulting boredom. It supplies novelty, excitement and, as a means of self-improvement, a legitimate way of spending money. Today hosts of persons seek psychotherapy for discomforts that a less affluent society would regard as trivial.

Rapid changes in conditions of life, too much leisure and money, and the substitution of role relationships for feeling relationships may help account for the popularity of psychotherapy. To explain its extraordinary diversity, however, one must invoke other aspects of American society.

In monolithic societies one form of psychotherapy dominates, such as exorcism in the Middle Ages. Societies like ours which contain a wide variety of subcultures, each with its own values and approved behaviors, tolerate a wide range of psychotherapies, all sharing some common values to be mentioned presently, but having special appeals to members of different subgroups. Diversity is further encouraged by our competitiveness, the high value we place on entrepreneurship and our thirst for novelty. For us, the new is always better than the familiar until proved otherwise.

The psychological health of members of a society depends on their sharing common goals and having faith in their leaders and each other. When conditions of life such as those I have just reviewed weaken these cohesive forces and the institutions supporting them, its members become demoralized; that is, they lose a sense of purpose and feel alienated from each other. At this point many seek to recover common goals and trusting human relationships by clumping into groups of the like-minded who offer each other mutual support. The psychotherapeutic dyad or therapeutic group is one such supportive arrangement for combatting demoralization. Psychotherapy can be viewed as a social institution created to fill the gap left by the decay of other institutions which gave meaning to life and a feeling of connectedness to others.

As institutions of American society, all psychotherapies, despite their diversity, share a value system which accords primacy to individual self-fulfillment or self-actualization. This includes maximum self-awareness, unlimited access to one's own feelings, increased autonomy and creativity. The individual is seen as the center of his moral universe, and concern for others is believed to follow from his own self-realization. Thus, psychotherapies assume that an individual can truly realize his full potentialities only to the extent that he permits and encourages those about him to do the same.

Self-realization is antithetical to the values of many religions which seek destruction, not glorification, of the ego, but American psychotherapy also downgrades or omits many secular values which rank high in other cultures. Our psychotherapeutic literature has contained precious little on the redemptive power of suffering, acceptance of one's lot in life, filial piety, adherence to tradition, self-restraint and moderation.

The primacy of individual self-fulfillment is well suited to a fluid, underpopulated society with plenty of space and unlimited resources, as America was during the first centuries of its existence. In such a society, the efforts of every individual to enhance himself advance the general welfare. An individual-centered value system, however, may be incompatible with survival in today's overcrowded America faced with shrinking resources and progressive destruction of the biosphere. Be that as it may, such a value system, which has its modern roots in Jefferson's dictum that man possesses an inalienable right to the pursuit of happiness, can easily become a source of misery in itself. For this has become, in the minds of most Americans, the right to be happy; so when they are not, which is inevitable at times, they suffer an additional burden of resentment and anger.

Moreover, the goal of self-realization can become caricatured as justifying exaltation of feelings at the expense of intellect, and disregard for the needs of others. This is exemplified by some encounter groups which seek to foster ecstatic experiences through intimate, highly charged emotional interactions (7).

While such groups pay lip service to mutual concern, it stops abruptly at the group's edge. Within the group itself the leader, under the cloak of respect for the members' autonomy, disclaims responsibility for the effects of his actions. Following his example, each member feels free to use the others to serve his own needs. Thus, such groups can easily become exercises in mutual exploitation and can seriously damage some participants (8). It is well to keep in mind that the true opposite of dependence, regarded as the ultimate evil by many American psychotherapeutic schools, is not autonomy but responsibility. In this connection, it has been pointed out that American psychotherapies are ineffective or even destructive in cultures such as the Hindu, which stress dependence and mutual responsibility (9, 10).

Turning from the values of psychotherapy to the psychotherapist, his power derives from his socially sanctioned role as a healer, which he achieves by undergoing special training. Together with his personal qualities, this enables the patient to form a trusting, emotionally-charged relationship with him. An American value from which the legitimacy of most psychotherapists springs is the continuing, if eroding, belief in science as the wellspring of human welfare. As a result, most psychotherapists derive their power from their scientific training. Of these, physicians have enjoyed a brief period of supremacy. Although physicians have always employed methods of psychological healing—often unawares, until the last century treatment of mental illness was primarily in the hands of priests. Freud was one of the first to assert the physician's claim to treat psychologically-caused symptoms and disabilities by scientifically-derived psychological methods. To make this possible, he assimilated mental illness to medical illness. The detailed exploration of a person's inner life, however, has no resemblance to any other form of medical treatment.

The dominance of physicians as practitioners of psychotherapy was not shaken until World War II created a demand that psychiatrists could not meet. They called upon members of two other professions for help, psychiatric social workers and clinical psychologists. Social workers have, for the most part, continued to work under the aegis of psychiatrists and to use their methods. Not so psychologists, who soon asserted their independence.

At first the therapies of psychologists were dominated by Carl Rogers, whose approach was an outgrowth of psychoanalysis, but in recent years behavior therapies with greater claims to scientific objectivity have gained ascendance. Just as Freud is the intellectual godfather of psychiatric psychotherapists, so behavior therapists look to the work of Pavlov, Thorndike, Hull and Skinner for validation of their theories and methods. Consistent with this intellectual ancestry, psychologists conceive mental illnesses to be disorders of learning rather than disease syndromes.

The entrance of psychologists into psychotherapy has led to a desirable increase in efforts to describe psychotherapies and their results in objectively measurable, verifiable terms. Without this kind of information, the field cannot advance. Nevertheless, despite mountains of graphs, charts and statistical tables, the fact remains that the connection between behavior therapies and laboratory findings on which they claim to be based remains questionable, and that in actuality most deal with patients' phantasies and reports of inner experiences. (Behavior therapists solve this conceptual dilemma by calling these implicit behaviors). Since most behavioral methods are relatively brief, however, and seem no less effective than analytically-based ones for most patients, their share of the psychotherapeutic field will probably continue to increase.

A final group of professional therapists, who see more troubled people than psychiatrists, psychologists or social workers, look not to science but to religion to sanction their healing efforts. These are ministers of religion, ranging from Christian Science healers to pastoral counsellors, most of whom derive their methods from Freudian, Rogerian or existential-humanist traditions.

To complete the picture, we must note that the enormous demand for psychotherapy, in conjunction with the declining prestige of both science and religion, has resulted in the emergence of masses of therapists with only tenuous claims to legitimacy. Many are trained in independent institutes; others claim competence in a particular type of therapy through having themselves undergone it; and some, like L. Ron Hubbard of Scientology and Harvey Jackins, the founder of Reevaluation Counseling, have attracted large followings primarily through personal charisma.

Finally, we are witnessing the multiplication of peer self-help psychotherapy groups. A few, like Alcoholics Anonymous, have been originated by fellow sufferers, but most trace their credentials to a healer who was trained as a physician or psychologist, and they continue to seek guidance from the writings of their founder. Outstanding current examples are Transactional Analysis, founded by Eric Berne (11), and Recovery Incorporated, created by Abraham Low (12).

In short, practitioners of psychotherapy now come from so many sources, while performing essentially the same social role, that perhaps they should be viewed as a new profession (13) whose members function to various degrees as healers, teachers, spiritual guides and sympathetic friends.

Social forces largely determine not only who become psychotherapists but also who become patients. It is customary to speak of certain persons as needing psychotherapy, but this is already a culturally determined judgment. Very few persons indeed need psychotherapy in the sense that their survival depends on it. Rather the term "need" is applied to those whose suffering and disability are viewed by common consent as amenable to this type of treatment. In American society these can be roughly grouped into five categories, which may be termed the *psychotic,* the *neurotic,* the *shaken,* the *unruly* and the *discontented.*

Genetic-organic determinants clearly play a significant role in psychoses, although their exact nature is still to be determined. After years of dedicated psychotherapeutic efforts, it now seems clear that psychotherapy cannot cure psychoses (14). Since psychologically-induced emotional states can aggravate organic vulnerabilities, however, psychotherapy can significantly ameliorate the distress of psychotics and help them to function better. Psychotherapy can play a similar role for patients with diabetes, heart disease, arthritis and other chronic organically-based ailments.

Psychotherapy is the treatment of choice for the remaining categories, in all of which the sources of difficulty are primarily psychological. Among these, neurotics suffer from symptoms which are persistent faulty strategies for coping with life, presumably resulting from deprivations or traumata in early life which distorted the normal process of maturation and learning. This group seems to evoke the most intense competition between proponents of dynamic and behavioral psychotherapies.

The third category, the psychologically-shaken, consists of persons unable to cope with aspects of their immediate life situations, including marital disharmonies, misbehaving children, and crises which temporarily overtax their adaptive capacities. Relatively brief interventions usually suffice to restore them to emotional equilibrium. Since persons shaken by current life stresses can manifest the entire gamut of neurotic and psychotic symptoms (15), and since all respond gratifyingly to any form of psychotherapy, they fan the competitiveness between different therapeutic schools.

The fourth category, the unruly, manifest behavior disturbing to those about them, but attributed to psychological causes rather than to wickedness. Here belong "acting-out" children and adolescents, husbands or wives whose spouses cannot stand their behavior and, of course, addicts and antisocial personalities. Some of these merge with the preceding category. The difference lies in the chronicity and severity of the disturbance and the motivation for help. The shaken seek treatment themselves; the unruly are brought to treatment by others. In any case, they are poor candidates for psychotherapy.

The fifth category, the discontented, consists of members of the leisured and educated classes who suffer from ennui or struggle with philosophical issues of existence. They shun behavior therapies and gravitate instead to psychotherapies with well articulated, strongly held values, such as Freudian and Jungian psychoanalysis and logotherapy. They also flock to the quasi-religious movements mentioned earlier.

For the sake of completeness, mention must be made of two small groups who undergo psychotherapy for extraneous reasons. One consists of trainees whose training includes exposure to the type of therapy they are learning; the other, college students with minor symptoms who volunteer as subjects in experiments on psychotherapy in return for such inducements as small financial payments or being excused from an examination.

Having looked at the values shared by all schools of psychotherapy, their practitioners and their patients, I should now like to turn, finally, to their conceptualizations and procedures. Beneath the din of conflicting claims and the kaleidoscopic panorama of activities, it is possible to discern certain characteristics which all share. That these may account for more of their effectiveness than the features which distinguish them is suggested by the persistent difficulty in demonstrating significant differences in their outcomes (16, 17). All therapies attract a loyal following, and I have yet to hear of a school that has disbanded because it became convinced of the superiority of its rivals.

To be sure, behavioral modification techniques seem more effective than open-ended interview therapies in relieving certain circumscribed phobias (18, 19), but these account for less than five percent of persons seen by psychotherapists (20). Many schools of therapy claim to reconstruct the patient's personality, although recent data from the Menninger psychotherapy research study suggest that this rarely occurs, even after extensive psychoanalyis (21). It probably happens occasionally, but its frequency is probably no greater than that of religious conversions, which have similar effects.

In any case, the least common denominator of all therapies, and the one on which their claims to success must depend, is their ability to help the patient reduce his suffering, smooth his social relationships and improve his performance. All aim to achieve these ends through patterned communications which seek to foster changes in the patient's cognitions, feelings and behavior. A brief review of the features shared by all psychotherapies that contribute to this goal may help to clarify our view of the field.

The success of all therapies depends in the first instance on the so-called therapeutic relationship or therapeutic alliance, in which the patient accepts some dependence on the therapist, based on his confidence in the therapist's competence and good intentions. The therapist uses his power to achieve three aims. The first is to enable the patient to discover new information about himself, both cognitively and experientially; the second is to arouse him emotionally, since emotions supply the motive power for change; and the third is to encourage him to change his behavior in the light of what he has learned and to practice the new patterns.

Schools of psychotherapy differ, in theory and in fact, in the relative emphasis they place on these components, but all exist in all therapies. Each of these areas will now be briefly considered.

The therapeutic relationship gains support from the therapist's training, his locale, such as a prestigious clinic, and from the congruence of his approach with the patient's expectations. These expectations sometimes may be greatly enhanced by the patient's knowledge that the therapist has faced and overcome problems similar to his own. This is the main source of mutual influence in peer self-help psychotherapy groups.

While these attributes determine the therapist's ascendancy even before the patient meets him, after they are face to face the main source of the therapist's power soon becomes his personal qualities, especially his ability to convince the patient that he can understand and help him. A successful therapeutic relationship in itself inspires the patient's hope, which not only keeps him coming through periods of apparent lack of progress or even of increased distress, but also is a powerful healing emotion in itself. His ability to establish a bond of mutual trust and confidence with his therapist also encourages the patient to try to move closer to others, thereby combatting his sense of isolation.

For Rogerian and existentialist therapists, the therapeutic relationship is the therapy; it is both a necessary and a sufficient cause of the patient's progress. They leave the patient free to structure it as he wishes and confine their own activities to facilitating his exploration and expression of his feelings, to which the therapist responds by freely revealing his own reactions. Such encounters are believed to promote personal growth, the ultimate aim of therapy. Therapies in the psychoanalytic tradition also foster openness by the patient, but make the therapeutic relationship itself an object of scrutiny. To this end, the therapist does not reveal himself, since to do so would interfere with the emergence and analysis of transference reactions. Behavior therapists, by contrast, while making a strong effort to mobilize the patient's expectations at the start (22), regard the relationship simply as a means for persuading the patient to cooperate in the techniques of behavior modification on which they believe their success depends.

In any event, the relationship enables the therapist to indoctrinate the patient into his particular conceptual framework and to teach him the procedures based on it. In conjunction, conceptual scheme and procedure have several crucial therapeutic functions. First, they provide a cognitive structure which enables the patient to name his symptoms and fit them into a causal scheme. Since major sources of anxiety are ambiguity and fear of the unknown, this, in itself, can powerfully reduce the patient's anxiety and enhance his self-confidence.

Conceptualizations of different schools differ in their views of causation. Since man is a time-binding creature who lives simultaneously in the past, present and future, all three perspectives are relevant. Analytically oriented therapies, however, place the main emphasis on historical causes. They search for past experiences which set in train developments leading to the patient's present difficulties, on the assumption that these will be relieved if he can rediscover and re-experience their origins. Behavior therapies, by contrast, stress the present. Although using a wide variety of techniques such as modeling, progressive desensitization and emotional flooding, all try to smoke out the immediate antecedents and consequences of the patient's symptoms or problems as the most effective way to overcome them. Finally, for many existentialist schools, the main source of the patient's suffering is his closed view of the future, so they direct their efforts toward widening his options.

Therapeutic conceptual schemes also differ in the degree to which they see psychopathology as lying primarily within the individual patient or in the communication network of which he is a part. Existential and psychoanalytically oriented therapies concentrate on the internal life of the individual, on the assumption that as this becomes more harmonious, his social behavior will automatically improve. Behavior therapists also focus on the individual, but try to help him modify his behavior, assuming that this will automatically reduce his internal conflicts, which they regard as outside their purview. In contrast to both these approaches, many group therapies direct primary attention to the interactions in which the patient participates (23). They see the patient as a node in a pathological communication system, whether it be his family, a neighborhood network (24) or a therapy group. According to this view, the most effective way of helping an individual is to improve the communications between members of the groups to which he belongs.

As new information emerges under the guidance of the conceptual scheme of any psychotherapy, it results in intellectual and experiential learning. All agree that intellectual insight is not enough. For change to occur, the patient must have a new experience, whether this be related to reliving of his past, discovering symptom-reinforcing contingencies in his environment, or becoming aware of distortions in his interpersonal communications.

Experiential learning implies emotional arousal, the second ingredient of all therapies. Some therapeutic schools see this as the essence of the therapeutic process. At least as old as Mesmer, rediscovered and later largely abandoned by Freud, abreactive, implosive and emotional flooding methods currently are at the height of fashion. The most prominent are implosion therapy, primal therapy, bioenergetics, transactional analysis

and, in the self-help realm, scientology and reevaluation coun-
selling. It is tempting to speculate on why emotional flooding,
like hypnosis, undergoes periodic ups and downs of popularity.
Part of the reason may be that these techniques are dramatic
and produce apparent marked changes, but then disillusionment
sets in when most of the gains prove to be transient. In any
case, all therapists would agree that some degree of emotional
arousal is necessary for the production of change in attitudes
and behavior.

Finally, all therapies encourage the patient to try out in his
daily life what he has learned in therapy. They do this chiefly
by providing him with experiences of success. These maintain
his hopes for continuing progress, enhance his sense of mastery
over himself and his situation and reduce his fear of failure.
The role of success experiences is most obvious in behavior therapies, which are structured to provide continual evidence of
progress and aim to have every session end in a sense of success.
Emotional flooding therapies, by showing the patient that he
can survive the full impact of feelings he feared would destroy
him, powerfully enhance his feelings of self-mastery. Psychoanalytically and existentially oriented therapies, being less
clearly structured, yield more subtle but equally potent successes. Patients who favor these approaches master problems
through verbalization and conceptualization, so the achievement
of a new insight or ability to formulate a hitherto inchoate
state of mind can powerfully enhance their self-confidence.

Review of the shared features of psychotherapies suggests a
somewhat unconventional approach to diagnosis. Instead of
trying to find the right clinical diagnosis, which seldom helps
in selecting a suitable therapy, it might be more profitable to
classify patients with respect to their relative predilection for
or ability to respond to therapies which emphasize one of the
shared features above another. We cannot do this as yet, but
I can glimpse the directions such an endeavor might take. It

would try to explore the expectations patients bring to therapy, their preferred type of success, their arousability and the like.

Expectations could be determined through inquiry about the psychotherapeutic experiences of the patient's social circle (25) or his own previous therapeutic contacts. Characteristic modes of help-seeking behavior (26) might also yield clues. Persons who seek aid by verbalizing their feelings and have strong motivation for insight (27) would probably respond to a verbally oriented approach; those who convey their need by somatic complaints might do better with a behavioral one; and patients with a strong sense of inadequacy might respond best to techniques providing early and obvious evidences of success.

Degree and nature of arousability might yield clues as to which patients would profit most from emotional flooding procedures. Would they be the most easily aroused, the most phlegmatic, or perhaps those who maintain a placid exterior while seething underneath?

If the analysis offered in this presentation is valid, it raises uncomfortable questions about the goals of training programs in psychotherapy. Until we have a rational basis for choice of specific therapies, one may well ask whether there is any point in mastering any particular one, especially since all have so much in common. Such a conclusion would confuse the content of therapeutic conceptualizations and procedures with their functions. Some therapeutically gifted persons, to be sure, can be effective with very little formal training, but most of us need to master some conceptual framework to enable us to structure our activities, maintain our own confidence, and provide us with adherents of the same school to whom we can turn for support. If any moral can be drawn from this survey, it is that every training program should expose the trainee to several approaches, so he can select and master those most

congenial to his own personality (28). The greater the number
of approaches he can handle, the wider the range of patients
he will be able to help.

REFERENCES

1. HARRIS, T. A. *I'm O.K., You're O.K.*: *A Practical Guide to Transactional Analysis*. New York: Harper and Row, 1969.
2. NEUMAN, M. and BERKOWITZ, B. *How To Be Your Own Best Friend*. New York: Random House, 1973.
3. FRANK, J. D. Therapeutic Factors in Psychotherapy, *Amer. J. Psychotherapy*, 25:350-361, 1971.
4. FRANK, J. D. Psychotherapy or Psychotherapies?, pp. 13-23, in J. H. Masserman, ed., *Current Psychiatric Therapies*, Vol. 13. New York: Grune & Stratton, 1973.
5. MASSERMAN, J. H. *A Psychiatric Odyssey*. New York: Science House, 1971.
6. HSU, F. L. K. Kinship Is the Key, *The Center Magazine*, Nov./Dec., 1973, pp. 4-14.
7. SCHUTZ, W. C. *Joy: Expanding Human Awareness*. New York: Grove Press, 1967.
8. LIEBERMAN, M. A., YALOM, I. D., and MILES, M. B. *Encounter Groups: First Facts*. New York: Basic Books, 1973.
9. PANDE, S. K. The Mystique of "Western" Psychotherapy: An Eastern Interpretation, *J. Nerv. Ment. Dis.*, 146:425-432, 1968.
10. NEKI, J. S. Guru-Cheta Relationship: The Possibility of a Therapeutic Paradigm, *Amer. J. Orthopsychiat.*, 43:755-765, 1973.
11. BERNE, E. *Transactional Analysis in Psychotherapy*. New York: Grove Press, 1961.
12. LOW, A. *Mental Health through Will-Training*. Boston: Christopher Publishing House, 1950.
13. HENRY, W. E., SIMS, J. H. and SPRAY, S. L. *The Fifth Profession*. San Francisco: Jossey Bass, 1971.
14. MAY, P. R. A. *Treatment of Schizophrenia: A Comparative Study of Five Treatment Measures*. New York: Science House, 1968.
15. TYHURST, J. S. The Role of Transition States—Including Disasters—in Mental Illness, pp. 149-172 in *Symposium on Preventive and Social Psychiatry*. Washington, D.C.: Walter Reed Army Institute of Research, 1957.
16. EYSENCK, H. J. The Effects of Psychotherapy, *Int. J. Psychiat.*, 1:97-142, 1965.
17. BERGIN, A. E. The Evaluation of Therapeutic Outcomes, pp. 217-270 in A. E. Bergin and S. L. Garfield, eds., *Handbook of Psychotherapy and Behavior Change: An Empirical Analysis*. New York: John Wiley & Sons, 1971.
18. BANDURA, A. Psychotherapy Based Upon Modeling Principles, pp. 653-708 in A. E. Bergin and S. L. Garfield, eds., *Handbook of*

Psychotherapy and Behavior Change: An Empirical Analysis.
New York: John Wiley & Sons, 1971.
19. PAUL, G. L. *Insight vs. Desensitization in Psychotherapy.* Stanford University Press, 1966.
20. MARKS, I. M. *Fear and Phobias.* New York: Academic Press, 1969.
21. VOTH, H. M. and ORTH, M. H. *Psychotherapy and the Role of the Environment.* New York: Behavioral Publications, 1973.
22. KLEIN, M. H., DITTMAN, A. T., PARLOFF, M. R. and GILL, M. W. Behavior Therapy: Observations and Reflections, *J. Consult. Clin. Psychol.,* 33:259-266, 1969.
23. YALOM, I. D. *The Theory and Practice of Group Psychotherapy.* New York: Basic Books, 1970.
24. SPECK, R. V. and RUEVENI, U. Network Therapy—A Developing Concept, *Family Process,* 8:182, 1969.
25. KADUSHIN, C. *Why People Go to Psychiatrists.* New York: Atherton, 1969.
26. HENDERSON, A. S. Care-Eliciting Behavior in Man, *J. Nerv. Ment. Dis.,* 159:172-181, 1974.
27. MALAN, D. H. *A Study of Brief Psychotherapy.* Philadelphia: Lippincott, 1963.
28. HAVENS, L. L. Clinical Methods in Psychiatry, *Int. J. Psychiatry,* 10:7-28, 1972.

Part II

THE PSYCHOTHERAPIES

2

Explanation of the Clinical Exercise

Hyman L. Muslin, M.D.

The exercise which we designed presented a clinical interview in order to elicit differing approaches to the treatment of a particular case under observation. Granted the limits of the exercise (a single introductory interview), our hope was that we could gather from each of our clinical experts a version of the treatment possibilities of the approaches of pharmacotherapy, psychoanalysis, behavioral modification, and group therapy.

The basis of the exercise was an introductory interview of a patient who presented psychomotor retardation and confusion, with feelings of withdrawal and fantasies of impending doom. She related these symptoms to the recent death by suicide of an older sibling.

In response to the clinical data, each expert related his version of a specific method of assessing the data (including, in some cases, the wish for a special interview) and outlined approaches that could be utilized from his particular therapeutic framework.

To capture some of the vitality of the exercise, we have abstracted and given vignettes of the actual interview so that the reader can participate, as it were, in the exercise and perhaps formulate his own set of approaches.

CLINICAL INTERVIEW

Introduction

The patient is a 60-year-old woman who enters the clinic for treatment of feelings of withdrawal and retardation. Her husband telephoned because of his fear that she was becoming more withdrawn after the death of an older sister. She was asked to report for an interview, which was to be taped, with me functioning as one of the Staff consulting on her case for further disposition.

She is an attractive well-groomed woman who speaks well. There is an air of distractibility and querulousness about her. Also, there are moments in the interview when she reveals anger, as well as other affects; thus, even while there is diminution of affects, there may be a discharge channel of affects.

The first segment of the actual interview is as follows:

Dr.: Okay. I think we can start now. Tell me a little bit about how you've been feeling right now.

Pt.: Today? Today's a beautiful day. (*laughs*) I feel fine. Uh, well, the last, uh, several months have been quite a strain on me. In my last interview . . . I don't think you know anything about the background at all, do you, of my case? Uh, my sister—on the ninth of July, uh, went into a woods and . . . and killed herself. Apparently, I mean . . . for no reason at all. And she did it in such a brutal way. Uh, she stabbed herself in the heart many times that, uh—that, uh—I mean, the thing was so shocking to me—terribly shocking and, uh, I guess, I just haven't gotten over that and I'm supposed to be one of the, well, executors of the estate. There's a lot of problems connected with it and (*sighs*) I just don't seem to be able to cope with anything anymore. Not even in my own home, let alone a lot of furniture and other things that I'm suppose to sell and dispense with or whatever. So I think that has worried me terrible. (*pause*) My brother called me the other night though and told me he'd help me through with anything that I had to do which relieved me a great deal, uh, of that worry. But, uh, in my home, I just don't seem to be able to cope as well as I did before. It's, uh—well, just little things, like going to the grocery store . . . cooking and cleaning and my little grandson lives with me and my daughter, both of them, it's very difficult for me, at this age, to cope with all that.

Dr.: So, it's been two months since the shock.

Pt.: It's been two months, yes. Do you mind if I smoke?

Dr.: And your own . . . your own internal reaction to it has been consuming you, then? You haven't been able to do your usual work?

Pt.: Well, I thought I was. I mean, I'm a person who loves to be outside. My life is kinda simple—I spend maybe three, four hours at home and playing tennis and swimming and then I go over and help my husband in the shop.

Dr.: Mmm hmm.

Pt.: I'm trying to hang on to it. Today, I—I did go out and played tennis and I went to the grocery store this morning and fried chicken, and my husband just wants me to hang on but it is just these things, I mean, they're—an ordinary, intelligent person should be able to—to do, I just, uh—I don't know. Maybe I fight against it (*laughs*).

Dr.: But you've been aware then of a feeling of lack of interest—something like a feeling of being withdrawn. Is that what you've experienced?

Pt.: (*pause*) Well, these . . . the whole thing is incomprehensible to me, I don't see, uh, why anyone as successful as my sister and with seemingly many friends and well organized and socially adjusted and all that—I mean, why someone like this should just . . . instantly fall apart in such a way. It, uh . . . well, it's just an enigma to me. (*pause*)

Dr.: That's what keeps occupying your mind, why-why did she do it? What happened?

Pt.: No-no. Not always. I don't say that. I-I try to go about my daily life, I guess, as well as . . . in fact, I think . . . the last few days, I have done somewhat better than I . . . when my husband called here, I think he was . . . he was in an excitable state too. And I think that maybe he exaggerated it in his mind—it could have been, I don't know. Uh . . . It seems to me like *I have to follow her.* You see, I have a premonition of this and, uh, (*pause*) I don't know why this should be . . . but, uh, underneath all of whatever I'm trying to do, it must be there because I-I seem to be kinda falling apart (*laughs*) that's all.

Dr.: You really feel different, then, since she died.

Pt.: Mmmm . . . (*pause*) Well, first . . . I mean, I was terribly shocked. I-I couldn't comprehend this at all . . . couldn't comprehend it . . . and, uh, then later on, I'm ashamed to say, I-I . . . she was extremely dominating . . . very domineering and promised my mother on-on her death bed that she would take care of-of her sister—I'm her younger sister—and (*laughs*) and, uh . . . maybe, uh, one analyzes this like she's abandoned me . . . that I feel she's abandoned me . . . (*laughs*) left me behind. I don't know if this makes any sense at all.

The patient goes on to relate that she was shocked at the manner in which her sister killed herself. She then expresses a concern that she feels anxious about *her* condition, that she has heard about shock treatments, which she associates with her state of confusion and perplexity. The next segment of the actual interview is as follows:

Pt.: And, uh . . . it's just a . . . it's just a mystery to me . . . this is the whole thing . . . just . . . but . . . (*pause*) I'll work myself out of this. (*pause*)

Dr.: Is her actual, uh, image . . . picture still in your mind . . . is she still with you?

Pt.: Well, I suppose, in a way, I have a-a feeling of unreality about it. I mean, I didn't see her body or anything like that—someone that I talked to everyday—she would come over and spend a lot of time with me. I mean, at least . . . but many times I *rejected* her because she wanted to come over and help me do this, and clean the house and so forth, and so on, and-and I rejected her and evidently, her-her friends rejected her in the end too, for other reasons, and I suppose it's partly a guilt feeling on my part.

Dr.: You felt that you had hurt her?

Pt.: Well, that I didn't know her, you see. It's just as if—I don't know if your have a person who's so very close to you, uh—maybe a brother or a wife or whatever—and you think you know them for all your life and, all of a sudden, you don't know them at all. I mean, what . . . this is just, uh, incomprehensible to me.

Dr.: Hmm hmm. You sound as though . . . as if you felt that was something that you should have been better about . . . should have known her more. . . .

Pt.: I should have understood. I mean, why . . . I was supposed to be the closest person in the world to her and she was a very—in a sense, at least, I thought—a very outgoing woman . . . and a very strong person . . . she's 70 years old now.

Dr.: How much?

Pt.: Seventy. But she looked like a woman who was about 55. She had been an actress and she wore a wig and she looked quite young and, uh—well, I just didn't know her, that's all. (*pause*)

Dr.: I guess, it's kinda hard not to feel some feelings of responsibility when something this tragic happens—even though, obviously, uh, there were things about her that you couldn't know.

Pt.: Uh, obviously.

Dr.: Mmm hmm. And she's still very alive within you. You said. "She's 70 years old now," as if she were still here, huh?

Pt.: (*pause*) No. She's been gone for several months but, uh (*laughs*) I don't suppose I'll ever be able to-to overcome what she did to *me*, in a way . . . I sense. This is a smothering . . . smothering thing . . . smothering thing . . . all my life and it's a . . . I guess, though she tried to do it with-with other people but she *made a very weak person* out of me. I think. I mean I'm-I've been totally dependent all my life.

The patient then adds that she had separated herself from her family and sister by leaving home and going to a conservatory to become a professional musician and teacher, but that she, the patient, never shook off the sister's influence on her. The affect in this segment is again somewhat agitated and there is some self-depreciation as she once again states that it is "ridiculous" for her to be in a state of distress.

Dr.: Do you find yourself thinking about her during the day or do you have dreams where you can see her in the dream?

Pt.: No. But, uh, I have a very—to me, it seems a very strange, uh, experience—my daughter's an artist and, uh-uh, we have a long hall . . . a 50-foot hall where my daughter has these paintings, she has-a still-a still life . . . of a gargoyle and, I mean . . . and then next to that painting is another abstract painting that symbolizes blood to me. I mean, it's just that kind of a thing and then next to this painting there, is a woodland scene—and . . . I love this painting of my daughter's and I often wondered what time it was of the day and when I walk by these paintings at night or even during the day and I look at this gargoyle, I asked my daughter-I said, "Penny," I said, "What does this gargoyle look like to you?" She says, "It looks like a Lewis." That was our maiden—my maiden name was Lewis—and "this has to be blood," I said and "this other painting of this woodland scene, what time of the day was this?" and she says, "Well . . ." she says, "Mother, this is about 11 o'clock in the morning." And this is the time that my sister did it. Now do I have to be crazy to think of things like that?

Dr.: Well. . . .

Pt.: Or is that just an association of-of a distorted mind, or what?

Dr.: I think she's still very much in your mind—thoughts about her.

Pt.: I even cross myself when I go down the hall and these *damn* paintings are there. (*laughs*)

Dr.: It's just the connection with her that, uh. . . .

Pt.: Yes, uh. . . .

Dr.: . . . you're frightened about.

Pt.: It, uh. . . .

Dr.: You're frightened about it, huh?

Pt.: Well, it seems so strange to me, that's all.

The interview then continues:

Dr.: Well, you mentioned another kind of frightening thought, that you're going to be next. (*pause*) Is that a very strong thought in your mind?

Pt.: (*pause*) I'll have to fight against it, won't I?

Dr.: Well, let's try to understand. How does that thought come into your mind?

Pt.: What? Oh, the-the idea of . . . (*sighs*) (*pause*) Well, my inability to cope with-with, uh-with these everyday things that are so . . . that really should be so simple and routine. I'm just beginning to feel that I'm dragging the family, that's all. (*laughs*)

Dr.: (*pause*) So it's connected with the feeling of being lost.

Pt.: I suppose so.

Dr.: Is that the way you experience it?

Pt.: (*pause*) Well, I-I-I don't have any explanation for it.

Dr.: (*pause*) Well, it's a pretty frightening idea to have that you're going to be the next and now you have to die—or you're going to die.

Pt.: Well . . . (*pause*) It doesn't have to be that way if I fight against it.

Dr.: But it is something you feel you have to fight against?

Pt.: Well. . . . (*laughs*) (*pause*)

Dr.: Hmm?

Pt.: Yes. I think so. I mean, winter is a bad time for me anyway. A very bad time because I-I love to be out of doors—of course, a lot of people do. I-I seem to be, maybe, in a sense, an escapist, in that way. I don't . . . to be out in the sun and the water and-and out-out of doors and then . . . I mean, with winter coming on, I just feel this is just the *last* summer . . . this is it, you see.

Dr.: Like you have to follow your sister.

Pt.: Yeah.

Dr.: Because like you say, she has been . . . she had been the leader for a long time.

Pt.: Yeah.

Dr.: Have you ever thought seriously about suicide?

Pt.: No. I think I'm very cowardly. I think when it came right down to it, very cowardly.

Dr.: You never had a plan.

Pt.: No, I never really had any plan. I haven't gotten that far yet. (*laughs*)

Then the patient gives some particulars of her relationship at home. The patient's sister who had apparently committed suicide was indeed the oldest sibling in a family of six; one sibling (a brother) had died directly after birth when the patient was 15. She was known as the good, obedient girl in the house and actually became withdrawn in her mid-teens; she denied any connection between this withdrawal and her brother's death. She recalls that she has always been somewhat introverted. Her sister and her mother, she states, were alike in their domineering tendency and, although the patient left home and returned (after her first marriage), her sister always lived with her mother. In the interview, she makes a slip tying together her sister's and her mother's death. The interview then continues:

Dr.: Oh. . . . So there's actually been two deaths that you've been . . . that you've had to face here recently, huh?

Pt.: Well, my mother died about five years ago.

Dr.: Five years ago.

Pt.: Mmm hmm. (*pause*) But I don't say that I-I brood on this all the time. I mean, I can't honestly say that.

Dr.: Mmm hmm.

Pt.: At least, I don't think I do unless I do subconsciously. (*pause*) Of course, my sister always gave me a great feeling of inadequacy, you know, of . . . a putter-downer, if you know what I mean. And, uh, maybe psychologically, I mean, I've . . . now that she's gone, I feel . . . well, that's-that's the story now. I'm . . . that's where I am and that's what she always said I was. (*laughs*)

Dr.: You feel more inadequate since she's gone?

Pt.: Well, evidently so. I'm not . . . I'm not taking care of things like I should. Although I have problems in my own home too, you know. I mean, my-my daughter hadn't been working for a number of months and this disturbed me. Hadn't been working for nine months.

Dr.: So much has been on you is really what you're talking about, huh? That's the feeling that there's been an awful lot of . . .

Pt.: Yes.

Dr.: . . . lot shoved onto you.

Pt.: And this little boy there—I mean, he's a wonderful little boy. He's nine years old and he has a marvelous personality and I love him to death but, I mean, it's just, uh . . . (*laughs*)

Dr.: Well, is it . . . is it really so that, uh, ever since you were a youngster—even with your mother and besides your sister—that there was always a lot of support and protection and caretaking—of you?

Pt.: Well, as long as I can remember, both mother and my sister disapproved of my husband and myself and the way we lived and the way we looked, the way we dressed —the kind of things we did. I mean, there's always been that aura of disapproval and, uh . . . our whole set of values is completely different and-and although I admire my sister in many ways . . . at the same time, I mean, I-I was an altogether different kind of a person that, uh . . . (*pause*) Oh, I don't even like to talk about it. Do we have to talk about it some more? (*laughs*)

In the final part of the interview, the patient goes on to relate with some hesitation that she has wishes to get away from her feelings and thoughts about her sister. She expresses the idea, once again, that she should not be having this strong reaction to her sister's death. Another reminder of her sister is her sister's material goods which she is to dispose of—a task which fills her with loathing. At the same time there are some possessions of her sister's which she has always liked. Several times during this segment the affect goes from overt anger at the reaction to her sister's death to an attempt to laugh at her (patient's) reactions. She also reveals again during this segment that her sister was always invaluable to her.

The interview ends with the picture, again, of an embittered, distracted, and somewhat agitated woman who has had no peace since the tragedy of her sister's death and who, because of this experience, has been unable to re-invest in her own life.

3

Psychodynamic Psychotherapy

John C. Nemiah, M.D.

At the outset, we should pay tribute to the individual who conceived of the title of this year's scientific program. He is to be congratulated for having referred to *psychotherapies* rather than psychotherapy. It certainly used to be the conception, if it is not now, that *psychotherapy* was what the psychiatrist dispensed when he was not giving medication or shock treatment. In my younger days, when I would occasionally make rounds with my colleagues on the medical service, it was not uncommon to hear the visiting physician say, "This patient has an emotional problem—give him some psychotherapy," to which I was always tempted to reply, "Yes, sir—t.i.d.? And s.c. or p.o.?"

Our internist, however knowledgeable he may have been in psychological matters, was indeed vague, not to say confused, about the nature of psychotherapy. For the word, of course, refers not to a single thing or entity that can be dispensed like ipecac or penicillin or digitoxin. It is a generic term used to denote a variety of maneuvers and techniques employed by the psychiatrist when, within the context of the special human relationship between himself and his patient, he is attempting to alleviate the patient's discomfort—a discomfort and a treatment generally best understood conceptually in psychological terms. It is within this broad definition of the word that we are examining a variety of psychotherapies, with the recognition that probably no treatment the psychiatrist (or any physician for that matter) engages in is without a major psychotherapeutic component.

My specific task is to focus on one aspect of psychotherapy—*dynamic psychotherapy*, which might as well have been called *insight psychotherapy, uncovering psychotherapy,* or *psychoanalytically oriented psychotherapy,* each of the terms describing either the origin, the basic aim, or the theoretical underpinnings of the treatment techniques involved. *Dynamic psychotherapy* is perhaps the least restrictive of the various terms, and has the virtue of hinting at the theoretical concepts of psychological functioning on which this form of psychotherapy is based. Let us begin by reviewing briefly these theoretical concepts as a basis for our examination of the tactics and strategies of dynamic psychotherapy, as well as of the indications and contraindications for its use. I shall be discussing these aspects of our topic in more general terms in the first portion of my remarks, and shall close with comments focused more specifically on the patient we have all seen together on tape—comments embodying my own clinical opinion as to the applicability of dynamic psychotherapy to her illness.

The word *dynamic* implies psychological structure. The human psyche is conceived of as having parts (or different functions) held in a fluid, dynamic equilibrium as the result of a conflict among the aims or goals and directions of discharge of these various psychic agencies. The most common, and commonly-used clinically, of the dynamic psychologies is that based on psychoanalytic theory. Stemming originally from the clinical observations and explanations made by Freud and his early co-workers in the decade before and after the turn of the century, psychoanalytic theory has reached, in contemporary metapsychology, a degree of sophistication and complexity that goes far beyond the needs or interests of the psychiatric clinician or the psychotherapist. For our purposes here the following scheme is sufficient.

Basic to all animal life, including man, are drives deriving from biological needs that provide an internally based impulse to actions that will satisfy and gratify the needs. In man, the sexual and aggressive drives, in particular, are a source of potential difficulty. Their uninhibited expression in action comes into conflict with the external mores of society, and especially with their internalized representations in the sanctions of the conscience and ego ideals, constituting, in analytic parlance, the *superego*.

A conflict is thereby generated between one part of the psychic apparatus and another, a conflict that must be mediated by yet a third psychic agency, the *ego*. The ego is a set of functions including sensation, perception, intelligence and the control of the sensori-motor apparatus, with which it must bring about the gratification of needs in such a way as to satisfy the conflicting demands of the various portions of the psyche. Of particular importance is the fact that the ego responds with *anxiety* to both external dangerous or life-threatening situations and inner drives, which it has learned, through the shaping influences of the social environment in childhood, will result in the punishment of physical chastisement or social isolation. In the interest of avoiding the pain of anxiety, the ego learns to control the underlying drives pressing for expression and gratification, and it does so through a set of ego functions known as the psychological defenses. These render the drives *unconscious*, and, therefore, unavailable to conscious awareness and expression in a direct form. Though unconscious, the drives are not thereby made inoperative; on the contrary, they continue to press for expression, and a compromise is often arrived at in which the drives, and the emotions and fantasies deriving from them, are allowed *partial* expression in a disguised form. These compromises are frequently viewed by the individual as alien to himself—that is, they are, clinically speaking, *symptoms*. Alternatively, they may result in behavior patterns or character traits viewed by the individual's family and acquaintances as unpleasant or antisocial.

Dynamic psychotherapy seeks to remove symptoms, change behavior, alter character traits and improve the patient's capacity to make human relationships. It attempts to do this by unravelling the strands woven into these psychological conflicts and compromise formations through bringing into the patient's consciousness those pathogenic elements held unconscious by the ego defenses. The general strategy of dynamic psychotherapy is thus easily stated, but the tactical maneuvers employed are often time-consuming and complex. It will help us to understand the nature of these if we review the historical development of the therapeutic techniques.

Freud, having been the originator of dynamic psychotherapy, is often credited with having discovered the unconscious. This, of course, is false, for the phenomena of unconscious memories were known to the Marquis de Puységur at the end of the 18th century, and the many studies of somnambulism throughout the early decades of the 19th century gave ample evidence for unconscious mental processes. It was, furthermore, recognized by clinicians, especially in the school of Charcot at the Salpêtrière in Paris in the latter half of the century, that unconscious memories of traumatic events could determine the form of psychoneurotic symptoms.

Despite knowledge of the pathogenic effect of such traumatic memories, they were not generally used in shaping therapeutic practice. Indeed, hypnosis, which could revive or uncover such unconscious elements, was used almost exclusively for symptom suppression or removal by suggestion. It was not until Breuer discovered that the revival of traumatic memories under hypnosis and the simultaneous discharge of the hitherto buried affects associated with them could lead to a disappearance of the symptoms that the so-called cathartic method of treatment was introduced.

Through his association with Breuer, Freud learned the techniques of catharsis under hypnosis, but soon, for a variety of reasons, abandoned hypnosis, and turned to *free association* as the basic maneuver for getting at the pathogenic unconscious memories and affects. He based his method on the theoretical assumption that the underlying unconscious affects and drives would determine the character and content of the uncontrolled, spontaneous, and freely reported associations flowing kaleidoscopically through the patient's conscious awareness. Freud's adoption of free association in place of hypnosis led him to the discovery of two new phenomena that became central for the technique of psychoanalysis, the first and most comprehensive form of dynamic psychotherapy. Let us briefly examine these two discoveries: *resistance* and *transference*.

First, as to resistance. In the course of their free associations it soon became evident that patients' thoughts often failed to flow regularly or to be reported on freely. There would be gaps, breaks and discontinuities in the individual's conscious perception of his train of associations, and the listening observer would be aware of similar irregularities in his patient's flow of speech. These discontinuities, Freud postulated, were the visible end-result of those ego defences responsible in the first place for the banning of anxiety-provoking mental contents from consciousness. In the course of free association (which allowed the unconscious mental events as free a rein as possible for expression), these events threatened to emerge into consciousness; therefore, the ego redoubled its defensive efforts to keep them suppressed in order to avoid the anxiety with which they threatened it. *Resistance,* in other words, was the visible effect in the therapeutic situation of the very forces of repression and psychological conflict that had in the first place given rise to the compromise solution of symptoms that dynamic psychotherapy sought to remove.

While the resistance created some obstacles to carrying out successful psychotherapy, the development of the transference raised even further difficulties. Like the resistance, transference emerged in visible manifestations arising in the course of the therapeutic process. Early in his work with his patients, Freud found that they invested him with many of the deep feelings and desires which emerged from their unconscious prisonhouse in the course of analytic treatment. These feelings, he recognized, ignored the reality of the therapeutic situation and repeated the loves and hates of earlier relationships, reaching back into the patient's childhood. As they emerged, their source remained hidden from the patient, who experienced them, initially at least, as emotions genuinely directed toward the therapist, whose image was thereby distorted in the patient's eyes to fit the likeness of the earlier person with whom the feelings had been first experienced.

With these introductory theoretical and historical remarks, we are now ready to focus more specifically on the nature and techniques of dynamic psychotherapy, although these are implicit in much of what has already been said. The most extensive and comprehensive form of dynamic psychotherapy is psychoanalysis, and we shall turn our attention first to a survey of the main characteristics of that form of treatment as it is carried out today.

As in its early days, free association remains the basic means of obtaining from the patient the information and observations necessary for the analytic process. While the patient is expected to talk freely and to report every thought and feeling, no matter how trivial, that enters his consciousness, the analyst remains generally silent, but actively listening, immersing himself in the flow of his patient's associations, searching for connections and patterns that will help to reveal the pathogenic basis of the patient's emotional problems.

The analyst is, of course, not entirely silent, but the comments he makes are generally limited to carrying out a few basic technical maneuvers. 1) He asks questions designed to amplify the patient's associations or to push them to the limit so that resistances may be highlighted. 2) He *confronts* the patient with attitudes, perceptions and patterns of behavior that he, the patient, has not questioned in himself before, so that the patient may gain distance on himself and view himself in a broader perspective. 3) Having helped the patient to new self-awareness, the analyst then proceeds to explore in detail with the patient the complex ramifications of the areas thus opened up for inspection—the process known as *clarification*. 4) Finally, when clarification has been completed sufficiently to suggest the unconscious elements important in the patient's symptoms and behavior, these unconscious elements are made conscious to the patient through the analyst's *interpretations*, which, if properly timed, are presented to the patient at a time when his defenses are sufficiently loosened so that his consciousness may be extended to include the previously unconscious material.

These, then—free association, confrontation, clarification and interpretation—are the basic tactical maneuvers of psychoanalysis. They are applied to two major psychological phenomena that we have already examined—that is, the focus in analytic treatment is on the analysis of the *resistance* and the *transference*. Let us consider each of these briefly in turn.

The analysis of the resistance is fundamental to the progress of the analysis, and the analyst must be alert to it and must be prepared to confront the patient with it and to clarify and interpret it and the defenses of which it is a manifestation. In this way, he brings about the ultimate emergence of the unconscious drives and conflict solutions that stem from early childhood experiences so that the patient may be the master of forces that had formerly driven him blindly into pathological behavior and symptoms.

Two aspects of this process must be made explicit here: 1) Since the defenses (and the related resistance) serve the function of preserving the patient from experiencing anxiety, analyzing the resistance and evoking the painful unconscious material behind it leads the patient to experience a considerable degree of hitherto absent anxiety as a part of the analytic process. He must, therefore, have sufficient strength of personality to tolerate the added anxiety without a serious diminution in functioning in his ordinary daily life. In other words, ego strength is a prerequisite for psychoanalysis. 2) It must be recognized that the application of confrontation, clarification and interpretation usually has only a temporary effect on the phenomena under analysis, for these are patterns of behavior and psychic structures of long duration and stubborn stability, and it generally takes a period of *working through,* of repeatedly analyzing the pathological material, before the patient can relinquish habitual ways of functioning and learn new and healthier ways of living.

The *transference* may be viewed as a special form of resistance. It is, as we have seen earlier, an investing of the analyst by the patient with often unrealistically held feelings and characteristics deriving from the patient's earlier significant relationships, particularly those of his first years of growth and development. The resistance aspect of transference is seen particularly in the development of the *transference neurosis.* Transference is a phenomenon extending beyond the analytic situation (as is seen, for instance, in student-teacher relationships) and consists of those feelings and attitudes which the individual brings to a new situation. In the case of the analyst, for example, these are often feelings and attitudes the patient has habitually held toward parental figures of authority.

These transference feelings are particularly important in determining the nature of the opening phases of the analysis. As the analysis progresses, however, and long-buried drives, feelings and conflicts are raised into consciousness, they will in turn color the patient's perceptions of the analyst with hues often quite different from those manifested in the initial transference. These constitute the transference neurosis.

What is important is that the patient may use his transference feelings toward the analyst as a means of *avoiding* the full recollection and recall of the unconscious memories that determine the transference neurosis, thereby posing an often stubborn resistance to the analytic process itself. The same maneuvers of confrontation, clarification and interpretation must be employed in dealing with the transference phenomena as in dealing with the other pathological psychic structures attacked in the analysis. The patient must be made to see the unreality of his transference attitudes and feelings (a process that requires a true capacity on his part for honest self-observation and distance from himself) in order that their unconscious roots may be revealed. In the transference neurosis is to be found the nucleus of the patient's pathological conflicts, and the analysis of the transference, therefore, has a central position in psychoanalytic treatment. With the full resolution of the transference neurosis—that is, with an unravelling and understanding not only of the oedipal, triangular relationships in the patient's childhood, but of his earlier, more regressive position of dependency on his mother during infancy—there comes a final ending of the analysis.

Psychoanalysis is, as we well know, time-consuming and limited in its therapeutic effectiveness. First, as to its limitations as a therapy. In its early days, analysis was used to treat patients with the so-called transference neuroses, that is, those in which the patient could establish a working transference relationship with the doctor. Practically speaking, these conditions were limited to hysteria, phobic neurosis and obsessive-compulsive neurosis. Gradually, analysis began to be employed in the treatment of a widening variety of psychiatric ills (including depressions and schizophrenia) and in a host of characterological and behavioral problems. It soon became evident that obstacles were inherent in many of these illnesses to carrying out the maneuvers of classical psychoanalysis, and a variety of modifications of technique—the so-called "parameters"—were introduced which forced the analyst out of his traditional role of listener and purveyor of confrontation, clarification and interpretation.

In recent years there has been considerable controversy over the use of parameters and the limits to which bona fide analysis can be stretched. For our purposes here, we will limit ourselves to a brief discussion of the indications and personality requirements for the employment of classical psychoanalytic treatment. These are eight in number: 1) The patient must have the capacity to form good object relationships, and must give evidence of having had such relationships in his normal life surroundings. 2) He must have psychological-mindedness, that is, he must be able to observe the inner workings of his mind, to describe them and to have appropriate psychological distance from them. 3) He must be motivated for treatment, recognizing the alien or pathological aspects of symptoms and behavior patterns and desiring to be rid of them. 4) He must be able to experience and describe emotions with a reasonable degree of ease. 5) He must be able to bear anxiety and depression without their severely impairing his capacity to function in his daily life or disrupting his relationships. 6) He must be of good intelligence. 7) He must be young enough to retain a flexibility and resiliency of personality. 8) He must be free of major environmental turmoil that would compromise his capacity for serene introspection.

We have spent a fair amount of time here on the theoretical background, techniques and indications for classical psychoanalysis—in part because it is the most extensive of the dynamic psychotherapies, but also because it is the source of other forms of dynamic psychotherapy to which it gives meaning. Let us examine two of these adaptations of the parent treatment.

First, let us consider *long-term, analytically-oriented psychotherapy*. With the tremendous spread of analytic theory and practice in the early 1950's, and their influence on the majority of American psychiatric training programs, analytic techniques were widely employed in analytically-oriented psychotherapy and were taught to hundreds of psychiatric residents. Literally thousands of patients were treated by these techniques in sessions of 50-minute hours once or twice a week, carried out face-to-face between doctor and patient, the treatment lasting many months, even years.

Many patients were helped by these measures, but many received no benefit or were even harmed by them, owing to the fact that they were employed indiscriminately, without adequate assessment of the patient's suitability for them or his capacity to utilize them. In particular, patients with borderline personality organizations tended to develop severe regressive transference reactions that often left them more seriously impaired in their functioning than before they entered treatment.

Because of this, a number of psychiatrists have, during the past decade, focused their attention on a critical assessment and definition of the characteristics and techniques of dynamic psychotherapy, and on developing more scientifically conceived and *briefer* forms of dynamic psychotherapy.

Not all forms of brief psychotherapy are dynamic, but there are some that specifically adapt the psychoanalytic model and aim at helping the patient to achieve insight. Among these are short-term, anxiety-provoking psychotherapy as developed by Sifneos (1) in Boston, and focused psychotherapy as described by Malan (2) in London. These are useful and teachable forms of dynamic psychotherapy, and we shall conclude our more general discussion with a few words concerning such brief therapy, as an example of current developments in dynamic psychotherapy.

By "brief" one means that the treatment is limited to four to six months, or 15 to 25 once-a-week therapeutic sessions. By "anxiety-provoking" is implied active focusing on the patient's psychological conflict; the therapeutic maneuvers are aimed at forcing the patient to discover and deal with the specific unconscious forces that are causing him trouble. The key word here is *focus*, for unlike psychoanalysis, where the doctor follows the drift of the patient's free associations, in this form of psychotherapy the area of conflict examined and analyzed is circumscribed, being generally limited, by the specific direction of the therapist, to oedipal, genital conflicts as these are seen in the patient's relationships and in the transference. The more regressive issues of dependency and pre-oedipal conflicts are consciously avoided.

It is evident, then, that the doctor is far more active and directive than in full-scale analysis or long-term analytically-oriented psychotherapy. The patient is, furthermore, under considerable pressure to work on self-examination, and is often subjected to a high degree of anxiety as he is forced to confront his initially hidden conflicts and impulses. It is apparent that this requires a good deal of personality strength to tolerate the procedures of confrontation, clarification and interpretation applied by the therapist. This form of treatment is, accordingly, limited to a relatively restricted group of patients.

The clinical criteria for the applicability of short-term, anxiety-provoking psychotherapy are those we have reviewed

in connection with selecting patients for classical psychoanalysis, except that the patient must also have a circumscribed clinical problem, which he is able himself to define,
and a detectable precipitant for his illness. If properly chosen
(and perhaps some 30% of people coming to many general
hospital psychiatric outpatient clinics are suitable for this
method), patients are able in a short time to learn a great
deal about their symptoms and the characteristics of their
relationships, the unconscious factors determining them, and
their roots in their earlier parental relationships. Follow-up
studies indicate that lasting changes in attitudes, relationships
and behavior follow a brief exposure to such therapy, and
there is a significant alteration in the patient's capacity for
both work and love.

Now let us focus our attention on the videotape interview.
The psychodynamic factors entering into the patient's illness
are unusually clear—its onset after the precipitating shock
of her sister's brutal suicide, the lifelong dependent-ambivalent
relationship with her, the marked identification with and the
repressed rage at the sister for her domination in life and her
desertion in death. Surely a patient with such clear dynamics
is a superb candidate for dynamic psychotherapy. And if we
view her against the background of the requirements for
dynamic psychotherapy I listed earlier, we find that there is
a precipitant, she is intelligent, appears to be psychologically-
minded as she describes her conflicts, is consciously aware of
her depression, and is suffering from painful emotions that
supply a motivation for self-understanding and for working
in therapy. She manifests, in other words, a number of positive indications for such therapy.

And yet, paradoxically, I should be very loathe to recommend
dynamic psychotherapy, at least as the primary modality of
treatment. If we look at her a bit more closely, we find that she
lacks several important indications for this therapeutic ap-

proach. In the first place, her seemingly close relationships do not have the character and strength of truly mature object relationships, in which there is a capacity to give and take love. On the contrary, her relationships, particularly that with her sister, are fraught with extreme ambivalence and basic underlying dependency, despite her reaction-formations against the latter. This is, furthermore, the center of her conflicts—issues over dependency, rather than oedipal problems, form the core of her difficulties.

Note, too, that in her relationship with Dr. Muslin she is often guarded, withdrawn and out of touch, despite his warmth, interest and human concern. In addition, she relates more by identifications than with mature *object* love. Her identification with her sister is clear and poses a real danger, I think, of her irrationally and impulsively attempting suicide like her sister— a danger at which the patient strongly hints.

Finally, I feel that this patient has significant difficulties in dealing with her emotions and she appears several times actively to avoid and evade talking about them. It is true that Dr. Muslin did not push her to do so and perhaps in a further interview or two she might more readily reveal them to us. But I wonder whether Dr. Muslin did not intuitively sense the dangers of probing too deeply, especially in the area of her aggression, which the patient seems particularly to avoid. She has, I believe, very little capacity to bear the anxiety and guilt associated with aggression; there are hints that she deals with it by directing it against herself.

All these factors lead me to judge that attempting to uncover her conflicts and impulses by dynamic psychotherapy, however clearly they seem to play a significant role in her illness, could lead to a deepening of her withdrawal and her depressive symptoms, and the danger of an impulsive, sudden attempt at suicide. If I were responsible for this patient, I should want first and foremost to see her on an adequate dosage of anti-depressant medication, and if I were then to try to explore the psychological ramifications of her illness, I should do so only with the greatest caution.

To sum up, diagnostically I feel that, despite the obvious precipitant, this is not a reactive, neurotic depression, but a more serious depressive disorder with underlying biological changes, falling most likely, without a history of previous depressive episodes, into the category of an agitated depression. If the more conservative regimen of drugs and psychotherapy did not prove effective, I should seriously consider electro-shock treatment.

REFERENCES

1. SIFNEOS, PETER E. *Emotional Crisis and Short-term Anxiety-provoking Psychotherapy*. Cambridge: Harvard University Press, 1972.
2. MALAN, DAVID H. *A Study of Brief Psychotherapy*. London: Tavistock Publications, 1963.

4

The Learning Therapies

Lee Birk, M.D.

and

Ann Brinkley-Birk, Ph.D.

Ten years ago it was usual, and five years ago not rare, to hear dynamically trained psychotherapists say that they referred few patients for behavior therapy for the simple reason that they encountered very few patients whose problem was "just a simple phobia" or other monosymptomatic behavioral problem. Today, however, there is a growing recognition that behavioral methods comprise the treatment of choice, or at least a valuable adjunct to more traditional treatment programs, for a wide and complex variety of problems (1, 2). In addition to the full range of phobias, simple and complex (3-9), these problems include severe obsessive-compulsive neuroses (10-14), childhood (15-18) and adult psychoses (19-24), hospitalism (25), mental retardation (26-27), depression (28-31), gender-identity problems (32), some forms of sociopathy (33-35) and even Gilles de la Tourette's syndrome (36). Recently behavioral methods have also come to play a relatively greater role in the treatment of psychosomatic (37) disorders such as migraine (38) and tension headache (39), cardiac arrhythmias (40-42), Raynaud's disease (43), chronic insomnia (44) and even, as reported in a pioneeering study, epilepsy (45).

What behavior therapy can accomplish within a pure conceptual system, or as an adjunct to traditional dynamic psychotherapy, is powerfully amplified and extended by deliberate integration of the principles of behavioral and dynamic therapy within a unified treatment model. In spite of the long-standing dichotomy which has existed scientifically and clinically between the psychoanalytic and the behavior therapies, there is no absolute deterrent to genuine theoretical synthesis of the two clinical-conceptual traditions (46).* Historical separatism has been the product largely of diverging professional traditions issuing from separate, seemingly contrasting scientific/clinical commitments on the part of the early Freudians and the early behaviorists.

While it is not precisely true to say that the principles and working methodology of each school can be reduced exhaustively to a common language or to shared methodological or ontological assumptions, it is nonetheless possible to describe the goals, techniques and therapeutic mechanisms of each school in terms of learning theory. From the point of view of learning theory, therefore, the insight-seeking methodology of the psychoanalytically-oriented therapies and the change-producing techniques of the behavior therapies form a truly complementary system: insight serves to uncover the learned, developmental origins of maladaptive behavior, and behavioral change serves to highlight the increasingly conspicuous discrepancy between reality-based world- and self-assessment and a distorted, idiosyncratic cognitive set which, if unrealized, would continue

---

* Moreover, all therapists who see patients with life problems and conflicts and try to help them by means other than or in addition to drug and somatic therapies are, in fact, employing *learning therapies*, or more accurately, unlearning-and-relearning therapies.

to support both maladaptive behavior and negative world- and self-evaluation.

The advantages of thus combining behavioral and psycho-analytic principles are further multiplied by setting the unified therapeutic system within a natural learning context, that is, within a social context in which interpersonal behaviors are consistently elicited, analyzed and modified. Working within a social system—peer group, family or couple—one can observe directly and *in vivo* the typical response patterns which comprise an individual's personal interactional repertoire for a broad range of stimuli occurring simultaneously and in sequence. A group of individuals, inasmuch as it is a wide-ranging and varied melange of stimulus and feedback, becomes the format for a unique learning therapy; in the context of a group, family or couple therapy format, an individual can learn not only that his behavior is socially-isolating, hostile, provocative, seductive or maladaptive, but also precisely what about it is so, and how it can be modified.

In this paper we shall be focusing on the efficacy of social systems as therapeutic tools in the service of *in vivo* behavioral analysis and treatment.

It is noteworthy that those who practice behavior therapy and behavior modification have, up to this point, typically ignored a significant portion of the available clinical data: the responses from others which are routinely elicited by an individual with symptomatic behaviors within the context of his own natural social environment. In desensitization, for example, a phobic patient customarily uses only self-report data and his own evaluation of the hierarchical levels of the fear-provoking situation. Moreover, in the treatment of ritualized, compulsive behavior, therapists rely almost exclusively on patient behavior-counts and on the traditional modeling effects of therapist activity. Maladaptive behavior is not an isolated phenomenon without social consequence, however, regardless of the contradictory presumption implied by the dyadic format employed by most behavior therapists. Except for the rare case of traumatically learned fears of nonsocial stimuli, clinically significant problem behaviors are generated and maintained within a social system, principally within the meaningful network of the patient's family, marriage or sexual liaison.

Because behavior ceases to be adaptive for the individual primarily when it ceases to promote interpersonal intimacy and personal comfort within the proximal social environment, it is maximally advantageous to undertake therapy in a setting where anti-social, distancing, troublesome or maladaptive behavior can be routinely elicited, observed and its social consequences realized. A compulsive handwasher, for example, characteristically imposes his rituals on all those who share his immediate living space. It is not infrequent for these others to observe some sort of ritualized bathing or clothes-changing as they enter the shared living space. Many experienced behavior therapists, therefore, do at present work adjunctively with the families of these patients, although neither primarily nor as a substitute for dyadic behavior therapy.

On the basis both of theory and our own clinical experience, we are here advocating that the concept of *in vivo* behavioral therapy should necessarily emphasize use of the original developmental social network—the family or couple—or an effective approximation of the patient's relevant social group in the form of an emotionally cohesive, personally binding group. Only in this way can the clinician make full use of the essence of the behavioral method: that is, direct observation.

Group Therapy

The therapy group is not at first a "natural" social group. Once it acquires "cohesiveness" and genuine social value for each of its members, it does become a powerful social group, in many ways natural in its function, although not in its origin. The behaviorally oriented group therapist does have reinforcement strategies at his disposal for facilitating the development of the group from a collection of individuals to a functionally and emotionally unified social group (47-52).

In order first to establish an atmosphere of honest, open self-disclosure, the therapist systematically reinforces all responses, of any type and from any quarter. Reinforcement takes the form of interested looks, nods or sounds, and affectively positive comments or interpretations. Once group members feel free to express themselves, the therapist begins to selectively reinforce interactional behavior and increasingly profound levels of self-revelation to the point where the group has come to expect and demand of its members a style of open, direct and genuine interpersonal involvement.

In addition to facilitating group cohesiveness, the therapist will direct his attention to the analysis and shaping of individual behavioral styles, including nascent tendencies toward self-analysis and insight. Insight-seeking questions about how, where and from whom patients learned particular feelings and behaviors function as discriminative stimuli for associative retrospection. This is automatically reinforced by immediate, gentle attention from group members who may be experiencing affective resonance with the disclosed reminiscences. If necessary, the therapist can use punishment in the form of negative interpretation or deliberate inattention in order to steer patients away from secretive, distancing behavior or to interrupt stereotyped and repetitive antisocial behaviors (52).

The behavioral therapy group thus becomes, in one sense, a natural social group; natural enough, that is, to serve as a suitable life-setting within which each patient's own, idiosyncratic, interpersonal style can emerge, be directly observed, labeled and shaped toward enhanced social effectiveness.

In fact, typically, in time, behavioral therapy group members *actually* become part of each other's most intimate social network, because they see each other outside the group. The pragmatic therapist does not punish the development of such extra-group contact or view it with alarm; rather he welcomes it, as a way of facilitating, through response generalization, the transfer of new patterns learned within the group to extra-group, "real life" situations.

In order to promote an atmosphere in which feedback is openly and constructively given, and accepted, the therapist must use the concept of modeling (53)/identification (54) over the full range of his own feelings as they are elicited within the group situation. This is possible when the therapist is deliberately open, warm, responsive and manifestly participant in the group process.

As patients' old, socially distancing behavioral patterns are consistently interrupted and thus punished under the pressure of group feedback, they are gradually replaced by more adaptive modes of interrelating. The group becomes a testing ground for these new patterns of social behavior, selectively reinforcing, shaping and progressively refining newly developed behavioral shifts. New social patterns become reliable parts of the whole behavioral repertoire as they are repeatedly and successfully used within the group and generalized to situations outside the group. Because they continue to bring the individual greater social rewards, these behaviors come to be a genuine, unselfconscious part of an individual's post-therapy personality.

It cannot be over-emphasized that a group format comes far closer to approximating a real-life social network than even the most interpersonally involved dyadic therapy. By focusing on the immediate locus of interpersonal distress primarily, and only secondarily inviting affective retrospection, the group provides "leverage toward therapeutic change" in the treatment of ego-syntonic, but socially ineffectual behaviors. The group format can be used to demonstrate with compelling force and clarity, in a way unavailable to the individual therapist, the social repercussion effects of an individual's manifest personality.

Family Therapy

Therapeutic work with an extended family (not infrequently spanning three generations) may be viewed as a special kind of group therapy. In common with ordinary group therapy, family therapy shares the advantages of operating within a context where the therapist has available for direct observation and intervention most of the behaviors which are personally and socially unrewarding for individuals within the group. For family therapy, as also for group therapy, these include both egodystonic behaviors recognized by the individual possessing them as symptomatic or problematic behaviors, and egosyntonic behaviors which, because of previously inadequate, faulty, disavowed or distorted feedback from others, had not been recognized as a problem by the individual.

There is one enormous advantage, in addition to those important ones already described, which distinguishes the group effects of family therapy from those of traditional group therapy: the family is a truly natural social system. It includes potentially all the significant persons who make up, or have made up in the past, the evaluative and distributive system of reward and punishment which served in some cases to generate, in other cases to shape or maintain, most of the behavioral patterns—adaptive and maladaptive—which comprise the total behavioral repertoire or manifest personality of each member of the immediate family.

There are two important strategic maneuvers which the family therapist can make in order to facilitate the development of truth-seeking, cooperative behaviors and the replacement of old, dependent, stifling, distancing or scapegoating patterns. Diagnosis and treatment begin almost simultaneously, for the family therapist can use the data collected during the initial, history-taking interview both to promote insight in the form of a generally consistent retrospective account which reflects the perspectives of all family members, and to point out, interrupt and shape the immediate interactional patterns elicited by the interviewer. In other words, the family therapist is operating with directly observable data of two kinds: 1) reflecting the attitudinal or interpretational style of each family member, and 2) evincing typical intrafamilial behavioral patterns.

The family history which is gradually developed by all the family members serves to expose the differences in perspective and interpretation which each individual brings to the account of a shared reality. An early goal, both diagnostically and therapeutically, is corroboration by all family members of a retrospective reconstruction of their common history; anything short of such a corroborated account creates a mounting pressure on all involved, the reduction of which, when skillfully handled by the therapist, serves as a negative reinforcement for cooperative, truth-seeking behaviors.

(It may be wise here to remind the reader that, despite wide misuse of the term, negative reinforcement is *not* synonymous with punishment. Rather, it is an ongoing stimulus situation which (because it is "negative") *when ended* serves to reinforce the immediately preceding responses. Thus negative reinforcement *increases* the frequency of responses while punishment decreases their frequency.)

A later goal of family therapy is the exposure and elimination of troublesome interactional patterns: father-son, mother-father, parents-children, sibling-sibling, and so on. In order to expose to view the focal problem area, the therapist should arrange to interview the family in various combinations. For example, he will see the parents alone, the children alone, the mother and the children, and the father and the children, as well as seeing the whole family all together. In some cases, he will elect to meet with the youngest children only, and to exclude deliberately, although temporarily, the oldest one or two siblings. This is often necessary because it is not rare for the oldest siblings to function as silence-enforcer or agents provocateurs for the younger siblings. Direct behavioral shaping strategies, employed by the therapist and gradually learned by family members, when applied to the problem interactional patterns that emerge *in vivo,* move the family as a unit toward the replacement of painful, perpetually angry, evasive or self-isolating behavioral ruts with warm, frank, autonomy-seeking-and-granting interactional patterns.

Couple Therapy

As the preceding sections have shown, the efficacy of behavioral principles is heightened within a group or social setting, the more so as that group is a natural group composed of the patient's own significant family or life partners. This is particularly true when the group is the nuclear family, or when the social system is the dyadic relation of the sexually-linked couple.

In doing couple therapy, one has at the outset the one primary interactional process to observe, but insofar as each partner attempts to involve the therapist in a personal alliance, a small-scale social system evolves. Using behavioral principles in couple therapy, the therapist first attempts to engage the couple in a typical two-way dialogue by reinforcing their looking at each other, talking directly to each other and finally interacting in a natural, unselfconscious way. This is done to expose not only the content of the problem issues to direct observation, but the interactional style as well. As in family therapy, it is important for the therapist to see each partner in the couple alone not only to form a separate alliance with each, but to observe the personality and behavioral style of the uncoupled individual as he (she) presents himself (herself) to another person. In addition, this affords the therapist an opportunity to learn in an early and direct way about otherwise unrevealed secrets: for example, affairs, fantasied affairs or unwelcome sexual thoughts.

When the characteristic stylistic patterns emerge, the therapist can reduce the frequency and intensity of provocative behaviors by negative interpretation, sometimes even by offering frank, affective feedback. The latter has the secondary effect of desensitizing the individuals in the couple to constructive criticism or feedback delivered with strong emotion. One of the goals of couple therapy is, of course, the resolution of conflict standing in the way of real emotional closeness. Another goal, not so easily accomplished or defined, is the exposure and elimination of dependent or neurotic over-entanglement on the part of either or both partners. This can most easily be done by exposing intimacy-avoiding, destructive or distancing behavior in operation in the immediate therapeutic setting, labeling them and progressively delineating their destructive consequences for the couple. The therapist can then contract with the couple: 1) to watch for and punish any future occurrences of symptomatic patterns, and 2) to work together toward learning how to replace old habits with new, more adaptive patterns.

Technically, this amounts to teaching the couple a competitive response system. For example, to shape the couple away from unchecked assumption-making, unwarranted imposition of feeling-interpretations by one on the other requires offering an alternative "I" position response by which each partner can symbolically define his own independent boundaries. Essential to the therapist's initial job with couples is watching for and reinforcing signs that the couple is engaging on a level and over an issue that is characteristic of their destructive or distant interactions. Once the clinical data emerge, the therapist can punish behaviors *in vivo* which he and the couple together agree are maladaptive, and begin to reinforce not only those behaviors which are more compatible with the couple's mutual goals, but those observing behaviors which suggest an increasing degree of objectivity in the couple, permitting them to act as their own referee during later difficulties.

In addition to reinforcing nascent harmonizing behaviors and punishing distancing, provocative or hostile behaviors, the therapist can assign graded behavioral tasks in order to promote a greater degree of sexual spontaneity and rapport or an increase in the couple's intimate involvement with each other outside the therapy setting.

Direct Sexual Therapy

Working with a couple to establish a greater degree of sexual harmony in their total relationship can require a different therapeutic style than ordinary couple therapy requires. In addition to self-report data from the couple, the traditional couple therapist can rely on data collected by observing directly and *in vivo* the problematic interactional style. The therapist dealing with a sexual problem in the couple, however, can only indirectly infer the character of the sexual problem from the verbal, non-sexual patterns which emerge during the therapy sessions. Sexual symptoms represent, in general, two categories of problems. First, is the class of sexual problems or dysfunctions which reflect an underlying, often unconscious, layer of fear, shame or inhibition on the part of one or both partners. Not uncommonly when the inhibition or shame of one partner becomes evident to the other, it is assumed to be the result of his or her own sexual inadequacy which the actually inhibited partner is presumably holding up for ridicule. When this happens, the sexual problem has already become a fertile ground for a more general marital discord.

In other cases, a sexual problem within a couple points to an unresolved struggle over mutual rights and obligations which happens to erupt in the sexual relationship. One partner may be using sexually uncooperative behavior to re-establish an otherwise unattainable balance of power in the relationship. There may be no real sexual inhibition, fear or shame which is leading to the dysfunction, but only the use of sex in a struggle for control, power or autonomy unobtainable in other ways by one or the other partner.

Whatever the cause of the sexual problem, the therapist begins his work by establishing, as the group and family therapists do in a more direct way,* a baseline of typical behavior, in this case data about the frequency and quality of sensual, sexual contact, as well as data about the external conditions of sexual behavior. When it becomes clear that there is either a sexual fear or inhibition in the couple or that each of the two partners is misinterpreting the other's anxiety, performance concerns or shame as avoidance or rejection, the therapist can begin to undo the learned, self-perpetuating, destructive patterns by asking the couple to suspend focused sexual activity and to engage instead in a graded series of mutually pleasurizing activities. These exercises follow an *in vivo* desensitization hierarchy, in addition to being themselves reinforcers for the couple's renewed pleasure-seeking behavior. Therapy sessions generally are used to report on the week's sexual activities at home, offering the therapist an opportunity, as has been discussed above, to observe directly the operation of the couple's feedback system, and to punish by negative interpretation or to subvert by direct suggestion any recurrence of the old, self-evaluative, self-critical or hostile interactional patterns. It is obvious that distortion or systematic misinterpretation in the

---

* Group and family therapists do this in a more direct way in that they are physically present during critical interactions. Sex therapists observe important couple interactions directly, but ordinarily do not directly observe sexual interactions.

feedback process or the presence of angry, provocative or distancing behaviors in the typical interaction is symptomatic of related problem areas in the sexual relationship.

When, on the other hand, a mutually unsatisfying sexual adjustment turns out to be camouflage for the couple's unresolved power struggle, a series of directive recommendations can be made to the couple in order to re-establish an equal share of control in the sexual relationship. In addition, assertive training can be used with the partner who feels powerless to cope with the other, except by indirect and ultimately ineffective means. This training helps to take the pressure off sex and to turn the couple's attention to the real issues in their turbulent relationship. "Fair-fight tactics" can then be taught on the spot during argumentative therapy sessions and can be used in combination with directive, pleasure-endorsing recommendations to give the couple a competitive response to their old self-defeating, mutually destructive interactional patterns.

✓   ✓   ✓

One of the strongest, most useful components in the methodological creed of the behavioral tradition is the emphasis on direct observation. Since a social system is built around its capacity to actively involve its individual members with one another, a group, family or couple is the immediate setting for the collection of directly observable data and for the operation of behavioral shaping techniques in conjunction with active, interpersonal feedback mechanisms. By combining the insight-seeking and change-producing techniques of dynamic psychotherapy and behavior therapy, respectively, within the context of an involved and involving, cohesive social network, therapists can significantly extend their diagnostic and clinical powers.

REFERENCES

1. BIRK, L. (Editor). Behavior Therapy: Achievement, Promise and False Promise. *Seminars in Psychiatry*, Vol. IV, No. 2, May 1972. New York: Grune & Stratton.
2. BIRK, L., STOLZ, S., BRADY, J. P., et al. Behavior Therapy in Psychiatry. *Task Force Report No. 5.* Washington, D.C.: American Psychiatric Association, July 1973.
3. *Ibid.*, pp. 6-11.
4. MARKS, I.: Perspective on Flooding. *Seminars in Psychiatry*, Vol. IV, No. 2, May 1972. New York: Grune & Stratton.
5. MARKS, I.: *Fears and Phobias*. London: Academic Press, 1969.
6. PAUL, G. L.: Outcome of Systematic Desensitization: II Controlled Investigation of Individual Treatment, Technique Variations, and Current Status. *Behavior Therapy*. (Franks, C.M., Ed.). New York: McGraw-Hill, 1969, pp. 105-159.
7. BRADY, J. P.: Brevital Relaxation Treatment of Frigidity. *Behav. Res. Ther.*, 4:71-77, 1966.
8. LAZARUS, A. A. and ABRAMOVITZ, A. The Use of "Emotive Imagery" in the Treatment of Children's Phobias. *J. Ment. Sci.*, 108: 191-195, 1962.
9. WOLPE, J. *Psychotherapy by Reciprocal Inhibition*. Stanford University Press, 1958.
10. RACHMAN, S., HODGSON, R. and MARKS, I. The Treatment of Chronic Obsessive-Compulsive Neurosis. *Behav. Res. Ther.*, Vol. 9, pp. 237-247, 1971.
11. RACHMAN, S., HODGSON, R. and MARZILLER, J. Treatment of an Obsessional Compulsive Disorder by Modeling. *Behav. Res. Ther.*, Vol. 8, pp. 385-392, 1970.
12. STERN, R. S.: Treatment of a Case of Obsessional Neurosis Using Thought-Stopping Technique. *Brit. J. Psychiat.*, 117:441-442, 1970.
13. BAILEY, J. and ATCHINSON, T. The Treatment of Compulsive Handwashing Using Reinforcement Principles. *Behav. Res. Ther.*, Vol. 7, pp. 323-326, 1969.
14. WALTON, D. and MATHER, M. D. The Application of Learning Principles to the Treatment of Obsessive-Compulsive States in the Acute and Chronic Phases of Illness. *Experiments in Behavior Therapy*. (Eysenck, H. J., Ed.). New York: Macmillan, 1964, pp. 117-151.
15. FERSTER, C. B. Clinical Reinforcement. *Seminars in Psychiatry*, Vol. IV, No. 2, pp. 101-111, 1972.
16. FERSTER, C. B. and SIMONS, J. An Evaluation of Behavior Therapy with Children. *The Psychological Record*, 16:65, 1966.
17. LOVAAS, O. I., KOEGEL, R., SIMMONS, J. and LONG, J. Some Generalization and Follow-up Measures on Autistic Children in Behavior Therapy. *J. Applied Behavior Analysis*, Vol. 6, No. 1, pp. 131-166, 1973.

18. LOVAAS, O. I., FREITAG, G., GOLD, V. and KASSORLA, I. Experimental Studies in Childhood Schizophrenia: Analysis of Self-Destructive Behavior. *J. Exp. Child. Psych.*, 2:67, 1965.

19. AYLLON, T. and AZRIN, N. H.: *The Token Economy.* New York: Appleton-Century Crafts, 1968.

20. AYLLON, T. and ROBERTS, M. The Token Economy Now. *Behavior Modification.* (Agras, W. S., Ed.). Boston: Little, Brown and Co. In press.

21. PAUL, G. L. Chronic Mental Patients: Current Status—Future Directions. *Psychol. Bull.*, 71:71-94, 1969.

22. AYLLON, T. and AZRIN, N. The Measurement and Reinforcement of Behavior of Psychotics. *J. Exp. Anal. Behavior*, 8:357-383, 1965.

23. AYLLON, T. and HAUGHTON, E. Modification of Systematic Verbal Behavior of Mental Patients. *Behav. Res. Ther.*, 2:87-97, 1964.

24. AYLLON, T. and HAUGHTON, E. Control of the Behavior of Schizophrenic Patients by Food. *J. Exp. Anal. Behavior*, Vol. 5, No. 3: 333-352, July, 1962.

25. BIRK, L., STOLZ, S., BRADY, J. P., et al. Behavior Therapy in Psychiatry. *Task Force Report No. 5.* Washington, D.C.: American Psychiatric Association, July 1973, pp. 11-14.

26. MINGE, M. R. and BALL, T. S. Teaching of Self-Help Skills to Profoundly Retarded Patients. *Am. J. Ment. Defic.*, 71:864-868, 1967.

27. ZIMMERMAN, E. H., ZIMMERMAN, J. and RUSSELL, C. D. Differential Effects of Token Reinforcement on Instruction-following Behavior in Retarded Students Instructed as a Group. *J. Applied Behav. Analysis*, 2:101-102, 1969.

28. LEWINSOHN, P. M. The Behavioral Study and Treatment of Depression. *Progress in Behavior Modification.* (Hersen, M., Easler, R. M. and Miller, P. M., Eds.). New York: Academic Press, 1974. In press.

29. LEWINSOHN, P. M., WEINSTEIN, M. S. and SHAW, D. A. Depression: A Clinical Research Approach. *Advances in Behavior Therapy.* (Rubin, R. and Franks, C., Eds.). New York: Academic Press, 1969, pp. 231-240.

30. SELIGMAN, M. E. P. *Depression and Learned Helplessness. The Psychology of Depression: Contemporary Theory and Research.* Washington, D. C.: Winston-Wiley. In press.

31. MILLER, N. E. Interactions Between Learned and Physical Factors in Mental Illness. *Biofeedback and Self Control.* (Shapiro, D., et al., Eds.). Chicago: Aldine, 1973, pp. 460-476.

32. BARLOW, D. H., REYNOLDS, E. J. and AGRAS, W. S. Gender Identity Change in a Transsexual. *Arch. Gen. Psy.* Vol. 28, 569-576, April 1973.

33. COHEN, H. L. and FILIPCZAK, J. *A New Learning Environment.* San Francisco: Jossey-Bass, 1971.

34. COLMAN, A. D. *The Planned Environment in Psychiatric Treatment: A Manual for Ward Design.* Springfield, Ill.: Charles C Thomas, 1971.

35. BOREN, J. J. and Colman, A. D.: Some experiments on reinforcement principles within a psychiatric ward for delinquent soldiers. *J. of Applied Behav. Analysis.* 3:29-37, 1970.

36. THOMAS, E. J., ABRAMS, K. S. and JOHNSON, J. B. Self-Monitoring and Reciprocal Inhibition in the Modification of Multiple Tics of Gilles de la Tourette's Syndrome. *J. Behav. Ther. Exp. Psychiat.*, 2:159-171, 1971.

37. BIRK, L. (Editor): BioFeedback: Behavioral Medicine. *Seminars in Psychiatry*, Vol. 1, No. 4. New York: Grune & Stratton, 1973.

38. GREEN, E., WALTERS, D. and SARGENT, J. Psychosomatic Self-Regulation of Migraine Headache. *Seminars in Psychiatry*, Vol. V, No. 4, 1973.

39. BUDZYNSKI, T., STOYVA, F., ADLER, C. and MULLANEY, D. EMG Biofeedback and Tension Headache: A Controlled Outcome Study. *Seminars in Psychiatry*, Vol. V, No. 4. Grune & Stratton, 1973.

40. ENGEL, B. Clinical Applications of Operant Conditioning Techniques in the Control of the Cardiac Arrhythmias. *Seminars in Psychiatry*, Vol. V, No. 4. New York: Grune & Stratton, 1973.

41. WEISS, T. and ENGEL, B. Operant Conditioning of Heart Rate in Patients with Premature Ventricular Contractions. *Psychosomatic Medicine*, Vol. 3, No. 4, July-August, 1971.

42. BLEEKER, E. and ENGEL, B. Learned Control of Ventricular Rate in Patients with Atrial Fibrillation. *Psychosomatic Medicine*, Vol. 35, 1973, p. 161.

43. SURWIT, R. S. Biofeedback: A Possible Treatment for Raynaud's Disease. *Seminars in Psychiatry*, Vol. V, No. 4. New York: Grune & Stratton, 1973.

44. BUDZYNSKI, T. Biofeedback Procedures in the Clinic. *Seminars in Psychiatry*, Vol. V, No. 4. New York: Grune & Stratton, 1973.

45. STERMAN, M. B. Neurophysiologic and Clinical Studies of Sensorimotor EEG Biofeedback Training: Some Effects on Epilepsy. *Seminars in Psychiatry*, Vol. V, No. 4. New York: Grune & Stratton, 1973.

46. BIRK, L. and BRINKLEY-BIRK, A. Psychoanalysis and Behavior Therapy. *Am. J. Psychiat.* In press. (To be published May 1974.)

47. SHAPIRO, D. and BIRK, L. Group Therapy in Experimental Perspective. *Int. J. Group Psychother.*, 17:211-224, 1967.

48. GUTTMACHER, J. and BIRK, L. Group Therapy: Can It Be the Treatment of Choice? *Comprehensive Psychiatry*, Vol. 12, No. 6, 1971.

49. BIRK, L., MILLER, E. and COHLER, B. Group Psychotherapy for Homosexual Men by Male-Female Co-therapists. *Acta Psychiatrica Scandinavica*, Special Supplement 218, 1970.

50. BIRK, L. Group Psychotherapy for Men Who Are Homosexual. A chapter in *The Cornell Symposium on the Treatment of Sexual Disorders*. (Kaplan, H. S., Ed.). In Press.
51. YALOM, I. *The Theory and Practice of Group Psychotherapy*. New York: Basic Books, 1970.
52. BIRK, L. Intensive Group Therapy: An Effective Behavioral-Psychoanalytic Method. *Am. J. Psychiat.*, 131:1, pp. 11-16, January 1974.
53. BANDURA, A. Psychotherapy Based Upon Modeling Principles. *Handbook of Psychotherapy and Behavior Change*. (Bergin, A. E. and Garfield, S. L., Eds.) New York: Wiley, 1971, pp. 653-708.
54. KOFF, R. H. A Definition of Identification: A Review of the Literature. *Int. J. Psychoanal.*, 42:362-370, 1961.

5

Application of Behavior Therapy

George Saslow, M.D.

To describe how the patient in the interview which you have seen and heard might be approached from the viewpoint of behavior therapy presents a difficult assignment. The interview which Dr. Muslin made for us is not a typical intake or diagnostic interview, but rather one which he and the patient were willing to arrange and to record to enable us to work with it in this special program.

The interview is different from one I would have used if the patient were being treated *exclusively* by behavior therapy. I would use the behavior therapy framework to deal with some features presented in the interview, but for other features I would use techniques that fit this framework only partly or not at all. Some of these other techniques have already been mentioned by Jerome Frank and I shall come back to these. My approach will be divided in the following way.

First, I shall mention some of the general principles and procedures that would be included in a behavior therapy approach. Then I shall discuss ways in which I might apply these principles and procedures to the actual interview observations. Finally, I shall prognosticate about some possible future developments if one were to use these procedures and principles in subsequent interviews with this patient. I can only guess about these in the absence of additional information.

General principles and procedures of a behavior therapy approach may be summed up as follows:

In the initial interview or interviews, I would focus on the patient's unique current problems or concerns as seen by the patient, not as I inferred them or guessed them to be. I would try to help the patient describe her problems as specifically and explicitly as possible in terms of behavior that could be observed or of such intermittent inner states as, "I feel discouraged," or "I am perplexed," or "I feel unable to cope," or "I feel sad," or "I feel angry."

Examples of the patient's statements that I would consider as her unique current concerns are: "This all happened several months ago," (meaning her sister's suicide), and "I want to take up my usual life again." Such statements were mentioned some nine or ten times in the interview; and "Over and over I say to myself, 'How could it (the suicide) have happened?'" and "I just can't understand how it could have happened." Such statements were mentioned some ten or twelve times by the patient.

I would then make observations of the unique features of the patient's problematic behavior, both outer and inner, and of the situational contexts in which such behavior occurs.

This is an essential point. Consider this example of behavior that can be reliably observed, but about which you must ask questions concerning the context. A man is seen running in a given direction. The observation of this behavior, say from a film or videotape, can be made accurately and everybody could agree about it. But, is he running because someone is chasing him? Is he running because he's trying to catch a train at a distant station that is about to leave in ten minutes? Is he running because he has just won a sweepstakes prize? Obviously, the running behavior by itself cannot answer these questions. If we wish to help the patient change the running behavior, we need to know the situational factors. From them we can design an intervention program. An intervention program which takes situational and antecedent factors into account, along with their consequences, can often be surprisingly simple, brief and yet effective.

It is essential that the patient's concerns and their situational contexts be described in everyday language and with as little abstraction as possible. Terms such as "countercathexis" or "libidinal vicissitudes" or "ego" get in the way of clinical assessment.

I would focus on occasions when the patient managed a current problem acceptably or effectively and in this way I would be recognizing and encouraging the patient's strengths. There is an old dictum of Adolf Meyer's that one should never talk about a patient's deficits without also mentioning his assets. Acceptable or effective behavior should be described as fully as problematic behaviors for a number of reasons. For one thing, constructive behaviors are likely to be more numerous than unacceptable behaviors in the repertoire of any one of us, and these constructive behaviors are more socially important.

Secondly, we have more effective techniques for increasing either the frequency or duration of acceptable behaviors than we have for eliminating undesirable behaviors. Undesirable behavior often has been reinforced at irregular intervals and consequently is extremely difficult to eliminate. A good example is gambling. One need win only a few times to get hooked. In the same way, temper outbursts can hook a parent into doing what a youngster wants even if the parent gives way only a few times, because the reinforcements are so powerful. Since procedures for eliminating undesired behavior come up against this unexpected and difficult obstacle, it is wise to recognize that we are much better at increasing desirable responses. Such techniques for increasing desirable behavior frequently are quick and simple.

Some recent work on depression done at the University of Oregon in Eugene shows also that when a depressed person, one not more seriously depressed than this patient appears to be, engages in activity which is habitual and satisfying, an elevation of mood results. Emphasizing those things which this patient can do well or which give her satisfaction is likely to be more effective than paying attention to her deficits.

Lastly, one of the most striking examples in our own field of the importance of practicing or even teaching constructive behaviors instead of focusing on removing barriers to desired behavior is the work of Masters and Johnson in the field of sexual malfunction. All the years that we have spent in trying to help patients understand the early experiences which seemed to be related to their sexual malfunction turned out to be less helpful than having them start with those things which they are able to do, such as examining each other's bodies visually and tactually and going from there to freer and fuller sexual functioning. This is reinforced by whatever possible learning and practice need to be done.

I should want my initial assessment of the patient to be parsimonious. By this I mean that I would focus on such information as is necessary for immediate, effective decision making. I might want to know only what to do the very next day or whether the person's life is in danger. Often it is possible to treat patients successfully for problems whose etiologies are unknown, with no substitute problems or symptoms appearing later. The patient's account of past events, which most of us learn to obtain first, is hard to verify. It may be largely fantasy; it may be irrelevant to current problems; in any case, the past is not reversible. It has often seemed to me that all that the patient needs is some kind of working hypothesis, one which doesn't have to be too solidly buttressed, but which connects plausibly the past events with present behavior, thus producing continuity.

I would not focus on the patient's negative feelings about herself or the patient's positive feelings about herself. In a behavior therapy framework, feelings and behavior are both viewed as occurring in relation to defined antecedent and ongoing circumstances and maintained by the consequences of that behavior. Behaviors are more easily changed than feelings. Feelings tend to change and become congruent with new behaviors.

Nor would I focus on earlier patient-parent relationships or patient-sibling relationships, which were presented to us so temptingly in the interview. Even if plausible hypotheses could be generated that related some current problem to the interpersonal behaviors and self-attitudes first learned in such earlier relationships, new behaviors, personal and interpersonal, are *not* counted on to emerge, in a behavior therapy framework, following careful description and clear understanding of earlier relationships, nor following ventilation or catharsis about them. Rather, new behavior is expected to emerge from 1) directly observing current problematic behavior; 2) specifying some different behavior that is desired by the patient; and only then 3) developing a program to convert the current repertoire or the current problematic behavior into the desired new behavior. An example of such past behavior which would not be used much in the beginning of behavior therapy is the patient's statement about her sister: "She always dominated me, I've always been dependent on her, as I was on my mother." It is tempting to focus on this and relate it to the patient's difficulty, but I would resist this approach if I were applying a behavior therapy framework.

In order to develop a program that could convert problematic behavior to desired new behavior, a daily log of some kind is generally used in this therapy. What might be included in such a daily log? You might work on one or two or three, but not too many, problematic behaviors. These behaviors and other events or inner states, such as feelings of anger or impulses to hurt somebody, can all be included in such a log. A record is kept of the frequency with which the problem being focused on occurs, and the number of times a day or week a necessary or desired activity occurs. Included could be the grocery shopping (which she mentioned as important for her to learn to cope with again), cooking, or recreational activities such as tennis and swimming. In other patients, one could have a daily log include records of the number of episodes of overbreathing in a day or a week, the number of episodes of heart pounding, of urges to hit someone, of discouraging thoughts, of thoughts about life's uncertainties or incomprehensibilities.

Whatever it is that you are keeping a record of, a baseline record is obtained of the frequency of the behaviors being followed. This record is monitored as often as seems appropriate. It can be every day by telephone report or any number of times a week during an appointment. Daily written reports have been found to be useful. Cassette recordings can be used by people who live several hundred miles away. The most useful daily baseline behavioral data about a patient's concerns come from the patient's own recordkeeping of the frequency of his or her problematic behavior elements. Such recordkeeping tells the patient the magnitude of his problem and, most important, whether or not an intervention program is being effective. Graphing such data over a specified time is extremely effective for the learning of both the patient and the therapist about the outcome of their program.

Other sources of behavioral data about the patient may also be used and are sometimes necessary. A spouse, for example, in addition to the patient, may be invited to keep an independent count of the number of angry outbursts against the spouse. However, two people who are complaining about anger being shown against each other may disagree quite markedly on the number of times that anger was shown or experienced. I remind you here again of the work of Masters and Johnson who found that two people living together in a marital relationship and saying they had no other sexual partners do not report the same number of times per month that they have had sexual intercourse. This would seem hard to understand, but it occurs.

Sometimes the therapist will want other people to give log data. If there are discrepancies, those too become part of the program of study and treatment. A family member keeping independent count of the number of times a patient accomplishes household tasks may be very useful (as, for instance, it is when youngsters have to divide up the responsibilities for managing a household and record who does this and who does that). A therapist keeping independent count of certain behavioral features during an interview can provide useful log data, but the most important data come from the patient, provided that you can elicit his cooperation.

An interesting example of a therapist's observations is the following. The patient was a boy of nine or ten who did a lot of scratching on account of eczema. The therapist worked out the following plan for obtaining data, not about the frequency of scratching, but about the duration of scratching during an interview. The interview would start and the therapist would then place a stopwatch on the table between her and the boy. The stopwatch was started at the beginning of a 30-minute interview. Every time that the boy scratched, the stopwatch was stopped and it was started again when he stopped scratching. Snppose at the end of the 30 minutes the stopwatch had run a total of 20 minutes; that meant that for 20 minutes out of the 30 there had been no scratching. If it showed 30 minutes, that meant that for 30 minutes out of 30 there had been no scratching. Thus, she and the boy could at a particular point discuss the question, "Are we going to aim at 100 percent improvement, zero scratching for a 30-minute interview when we are discussing difficult things in your life, or will 90 percent of the time be okay?" They both agreed that 90 percent of the time was a good outcome to be settled for. Like records of frequencies, records of duration can be both simple and very useful.

Counting behavior features *during* an interview has some special advantages. Such counts may show the priorities that the patient gives to each of several concerns. For example, in the interview we saw, the patient mentioned nine or ten times her desire to resume her ordinary daily activity. Now, let's suppose that you are having a fourth or fifth interview with her, and you are used to making these observations and keeping them in your head or somehow scratching them somewhere on your memory tablet. Suppose that the interview count of this behavior now becomes zero. You have made an important observation about what has happened with respect to the frequency with which she experiences concern about resuming her ordinary activities. She also mentioned about the same number of times how puzzled she was about her sister's extraordinary, cruel and barbarous method (as it seemed to her) of committing suicide. You might notice that such references changed in frequency from interview to interview.

Counting specific behavior features during an interview may also suggest ways in which the therapist can strengthen a patient's behavior. For example, one could reinforce every time the patient reported resuming a daily activity like "I fried chicken yesterday," by saying "Well, that sounds fine." You may pay specific attention to those very simple things.

Such counts during an interview can also establish a baseline which can be compared in later interviews with the consequences of any planned treatment program that you set up. Such counts may also show patient strengths which can be encouraged and increased. For example, with a difficult, unassertive patient, suppose you notice that the patient once in a while sticks up for himself and you want to increase that reaction by agreeing with the patient. You have got the observations in the interview, and because you are a rather important figure for the patient, it may be that the patient will increase the number of times he will differ with you.

Another aspect of the use of counting that is not widely appreciated in that any identifiable, non-continuous behavior, feeling, intention, thought sequence or fantasy can be counted. Even children can be taught to count their impulses to hit a classmate. Let me give you a complicated example. A surgeon had the urge to pass every driver on the road. Even if the driver was on the left, he would want to pass on the right to get ahead of him. If the driver didn't let him do that, he would finally pass him, stop and get out. He was, by the way, almost seven feet tall. He would tower over the smaller driver in the other car and give him hell for not letting him pass. He came to recognize that this was one of a number of related behaviors which were alienating many people from him. I proposed to him, somewhat to his amusement, as we began working together that he record each day the number of urges he had to pass every driver on the road. In addition, I asked him to record the number of times a day he identified an urge to pass a driver on the road, but did not in fact pass the car. Thus, he was asked to record two behavioral features—one he no longer desired and could master, and one he no longer desired, but did not master. The undesired behavior I labeled a "learning opportunity" rather than an error, thinking that if he really wanted to change his behavior every time he messes up, the mess-up can be labeled a chance to learn how to do the thing better. So, he was to count the number of learning opportunities, the urges to pass a driver on the road which he carried out in action, and he was also to count the number of times that he mastered such a learning opportunity. He was to do this for a number of days and then report. He started this enterprise with great skepticism.

Before I tell you the outcome of that particular bit of counting, I want to mention that the number of kinds of complex behaviors and non-continuous inner states which decrease or increase. in frequency as desired by the person as a result of regular simple counting of just this sort is not known at the present time. People remain surprised by how many kinds of behavior and inner states can be dealt with in this way. It has been estimated by Ogden Lindsley, who first introduced emphasis on the counting of inner states, that up to 20 percent of the people who use this device move the desired frequency of a behavioral feature that bothers them in the direction they want it to go, often very quickly and often despite years of its occurrence. Thus it was with this surgeon. After three days he called me up and said, "I can't believe it; I thought you were playing a game with me. I didn't know what the game was. But this passing cars is down by about 80 or 90 percent. I've never been able to do that before." He didn't have to agree with me, he didn't have to believe in what I proposed. If he would only do it, or be willing to try to do it, he might find a surprising result.

The daily log must contain more than frequency counts or other numerical measures of the problematic behavior. The patient is asked to provide anecdotal information which places the problematic behavior in some kind of situational context. Anecdotal information includes events or behavioral sequences antecedent to the problematic bit of behavior, accompanying it, or consequent upon it. Such information helps decide the next steps of the treatment program. It helps focus attention upon a problem now seen as having higher priority than the one originally presented. You find that you often change these priorities as one problem after another drops out of view. Such anecdotal information may suggest consequences of a given bit of behavior which are less punishing or less reinforcing, so that the frequency of the behavior will change.

With the patient in the interview that we saw, you will recall her extraordinary description of three paintings at the end of a long hallway, which would be the last thing she looked at when she would go out of the apartment. These paintings had a special significance for her, particularly the last one of the morning woodland scene which her daughter, an artist, had painted that seemed to prophesy the time when the patient's older sister killed herself. As she walked out of the apartment, our patient would cross herself. What we have learned is that as she walks out of her apartment and sees these paintings, she has thoughts about her sister's incomprehensible suicide. After helping her put these two things together, one could discuss with her the possibility of placing the paintings in another sequence. She could be asked if she would like to try placing the paintings at the beginning of the hallway or if she would like to remove the paintings and observe what happens. All she is doing is counting the frequency of her thoughts, "How could my sister have done something so incomprehensible?" You are not threatening her with examining her old relationships as would be done with a psychoanalytic approach.

To help pinpoint a patient's concerns, the interviewer should not be too concerned at first about a precise diagnostic category. A diagnostic category by definition lumps patients together. It fails to be sufficiently patient-specific. I'm saying that *at the beginning* that's not wise to do. The interviewer needs rather to facilitate the disclosure and identification of the patient's concerns in a specific way by frequent paraphrasing of short segments of the patient's messages, mostly with exploratory responses, to encourage further specificity. (By an exploratory response I mean what most of us have been taught to call an open-ended response: "And so?" "And then?" "And what else?" "Tell me some more.") It does not help to pinpoint the concerns that need to be worked with if the interviewer shows agreement too soon with the major points made by the patient. Nor does it help to pinpoint the patient's concerns if an interviewer assumes that he understands the patient's motivations or emotional state. It is tempting for us to do that because of our experiences with other patients, but it really blocks our getting patient-specific information.

When intervention programs are to be decided on, what are the most solidly based data on which to base a choice of an intervention program? Nothing is likely to be as close to the patient's concerns as the patient's own direct daily observations of his behavior and inner states. Early parent-child interactions, even if well disclosed and clarified, cannot necessarily be taken as accurate, relevant, or even useful. The family's perceptions of the patient's behavior may have important omissions and distortions. The therapist's prior knowledge of what seemed to be similar cases may be far from patient-specific. The patient's behavior during interview may omit significant acceptable behavior or undesirable behavior evident in other solitary or social contexts. In an interview with a therapist, the patient's verbal reports of his behavior may have significant omissions as compared to a regular daily log of specific features of the patient's behavior kept by the patient himself or herself, despite the various difficulties which are easy for us to list. That's the place it seems to me to begin—with the patient's own regular observations of his behavior and inner states. If there are important discrepancies between the patient's behavior outside and his behavior with me as a therapist, that's something to identify, examine and work on.

When may a therapist start an intervention program for altering problematic behavior? One obvious criterion is when the therapist perceives an emergency. In the case of this patient, the husband called two months after the suicide of the sister and made the appointment. Although the patient describes him as excitable, nevertheless that sequence might have led a therapist to decide, "This is an emergency and I had better do something right away." This something might be as simple as, "I want you to phone me tonight," or "I want you to see me tomorrow," or "I want you and your husband to see me tomorrow." A similar emergency often met with in college student health work involves a student suddenly appearing in a counselor's office, overwhelmed by being several course papers behind, talking of dropping out, talking of discouragement and suicide. This is a time for intervention.

Another main criterion for deciding it is time for an intervention occurs when baseline records of behavioral features that the patient wants to develop or strengthen and of features that are undesired and important are available over an appropriate number of days. Such baseline data may not be available in the first interview or even in one or two, in which case you simply have to wait until it is available if there is no emergency and you wish to plan a solid intervention.

Let us now suppose that a behavioral treatment program has been decided on. It includes three things: 1) an explicitly stated and desired behavioral outcome. "Here is what I want to have happen"; 2) identification of the current behavioral repertoire that is relevant to that outcome, that is, what does the patient have as assets to work with that are somewhere close to the desired outcome? and 3) explicit identification of steps to get from the current repertoire to the desired repertoire.

Here is an example which covers these three points. The outcome desired by a 35-year-old, attractive, intelligent, married woman was sustained, expressive, meaningful, woman-man relationships without deliberate sexual arousal and without sexual intercourse. In her current repertoire, she had a solid marital relationship, effective seductive behavior, strong affectionate and sexual feelings, strong and varied professional interests similar to those of male colleagues at work. Some specified steps which we agreed on to work towards where she wanted to be were: she was to initiate various kinds of woman-man interaction with men colleagues, to set limits on her dress, grooming, seductive behavior, the interaction setting, physical contact and duration of the interactions in ways that we both discussed explicitly. We kept a record of specific aspects of her conduct, of specific feelings and outcomes. This was generally done by a written diary, the record keeping mode which she preferred, of exactly what happened as we carried out this program, with periodic interviews for monitoring, review and improvement of the intervention program.

How can we help a patient move towards behavior that is more desired than current behavior? You have to search for reinforcers, states of affairs that after a specific bit of behavior increase the likelihood of that behavior occurring again. Reinforcers are not just food or goodies. They are highly idiosyncratic; that is why they have to be searched for. Moreover, they tend to lose effectiveness if overused. So, several reinforcers used at different times are more helpful in increasing a desired behavioral feature than just one. Examples of reinforcers can be material rewards, such as points to accumulate towards something especially desirable, like a vacation trip six months hence; social rewards; or behavioral rewards, which can include the therapist's behavior.

Sometimes what needs to be done is surprisingly effective though extremely simple. For example, I remember a woman patient who complained that for years she had never been able to get her daily household tasks started and done in any reasonable time because she would pick up the morning paper and become absorbed in it, while the breakfast dishes of a family of six would go undone. Pretty soon the morning was gone. That she enjoyed reading the paper a lot more than she enjoyed doing the dishes was the message of her behavior. Asking if she would try the reverse sequence—to read the paper only after she had done the dishes or worked at them for a certain number of minutes—took advantage of the fact that in her repertoire she had highly satisfying behavior (reading the paper) well practiced, easy and congenial, which could be used to move her in a direction not so congenial (getting the dishes done) which nevertheless she felt she ought to achieve. This general principle—that behavior of higher frequency can be used as a reinforcer to alter the frequency of another behavior that is a target of an intervention program—is called the Premack principle, after the person who first described it. This is what I meant when I said that sometimes the procedures which need to be undertaken in a behavior therapy approach may be very powerful, may take advantage of the fact that our behavior is modified by its consequences, and at the same time are easily possible with successful outcome.

I remember another situation in which sexual activity was difficult and distasteful for a young married woman who had grown up in a highly inhibited family. It turned out that what would reinforce her in making sexual life more satisfying for her and her husband was that, a few minutes after sexual intercourse, she would spend 30 minutes downstairs by herself, sitting before the fire. That was her idiosyncratic reinforcer which moved her behavior in the direction that they both wanted.

The search for a reinforcer that will support new behavior is not always successful. Sometimes no change in behavior that makes any sense to an outsider seems likely to occur. A possible explanation may be that nothing is as sensible as the behavior that is bothering the outsider. For instance, in a recent report, there was a patient who repeatedly landed in the hospital with some kind of self-inflicted injury. It turned out that the patient had various handicaps which made him utterly unacceptable to his family. He had no place to go and the only place where he found any kind of social companionship and satisfaction was in the hospital. It wasn't surprising that repeatedly the hospital found him bouncing back with one or another kind of factitious lesion.

How might some of these principles and procedures be applied to the videotaped interview data that we have seen? From a behavior therapy framework, I would have handled the interview somewhat differently than Dr. Muslin did, though, of course, I recognize that he prepared this interview for a specific purpose. I would have followed the patient's leads very carefully, especially whenever she mentioned a current concern or acceptable behavior, such as "I can't cope," or "I did go shopping once," or "I did play tennis this week," or "It's so incomprehensible," (about her sister). I would show special attention to such leads. I would have paraphrased carefully these several problems and especially the current ones. I would have summarized longer portions of her communication a few times during the interview, again focusing especially on current concerns or inner states which occurred with high frequency. Then I would have tried to identify her concerns in ways that are specific to her and would try to find out in relation to the concerns that are specifically hers the answers to such questions as, "What would you like to change right now?" and "What would make you feel better right now?" Thus we would begin to define directions in which we could both agree to move.

With the patient's participation, I would try to reach agreement on a set of priorities with respect to her current problems, since I would not expect to deal with all of them. I would have to decide, for example, where on a priority list to put coping versus not coping ("It's so hard to understand what happened," "I'm afraid of what will happen to me,") in relation to her premonition that she, too, must die. I would have reinforced her for her improved coping behavior, but the interviewer in this interview, intent upon another objective, chiefly reinforced her references to the past. Within a behavior therapy framework, I would tend to ignore her deficits and pay attention to those things that have to do with competency. I would not have tried to guess at her motives or how she should feel. She appeared to ignore nearly every attempt of the interviewer when he behaved in these ways.

Given the existing interview, there are behavioral features that can be identified and from which choices can be made in starting to work with the patient. It is noticeable that the patient could move easily (a measure of the degree of psychomotor retardation), she smiles, she laughs, she has her head in her hands 14 times, her voice fades away nine times, she fumbles with her hands and glasses nine times, there are more than three long silences, she sighs a number of times. Some of these non-verbal changes appear to follow the interviewer's focusing on the past. The patient defines coping with current home situations as a problem—shopping for groceries, cooking, having her daughter at home out of work for nine months and having a healthy nine-year-old grandson who is difficult for her in ways not yet specified. She defines coping with her dead sister's designation of her as the estate executrix as a problem. The brothers want some of the sister's possessions ("I can't even enter her apartment." "I've got that car."). She has begun to resume satisfying or necessary activities such as shopping, cooking and tennis. One could aim at increasing the frequency of these activities. She mentioned at least seven times, "My sister's final act puzzles me. How could she do it?" This, in most instances, was usually in response to the interviewer's directing attention to the past.

There was an important kind of discrepancy between two behaviors in the interview. Her *perception* of herself was that, "I was a good girl, I was good for mother, I was dominated by mother. I did what she wanted, I didn't leave home to go to college. I was dominated by my sister Jean." But her *description* of her behavior is not at all that of a submissive or dependent person. She mentioned that "I've been married (in my

second marriage) for 32 years. I am different from my mother
and sister. They both disapproved of my 32-year-old marriage.
My husband and I have values different from those of my family, we look different, we dress differently, I rejected my sister
often." Here is a discrepancy between self-perception and behavior, always important to work with, which is available in the
interview.

She had complex emotions regarding her sister. "How could
she do it? How could she do it that way? I don't understand
her. I feel lost. I feel abandoned by her. I feel inadequate. I
don't want to think about her. I often rejected her. I feel a premonition I'll die next. I have to follow her. The whole thing is
ridiculous; those paintings on the wall." All of these are feelings
about her sister which would be important to work with. She
said, "I exaggerate things out of all proportion." She wondered
as she sat next to a patient in the waiting room before she had
talked with Dr. Muslin, "Will I have to have electroshock therapy?" "My husband was excited when he called." "My sister
was dramatic—she was an actress. Was she real?" There is a
whole family tradition of dramatic excitability, which is part of
what she talks about.

How might we make use of such interview data as these? The
patient could, for example, be asked to keep a daily record of
her valued and necessary activities, such as helping her husband
in the bookshop, shopping, cooking, swimming, playing tennis.
We would be focusing on what the patient can do, not on her
deficits. It has been found, over and over again, that persons
who continue their ordinary, necessary and often satisfying activities can work on their deficits just as well as they can work
on their other problems. I would never think of interrupting her
ordinary activities in order to concentrate exclusively on her
problems. Furthermore, one of the important principles of how
reinforcers can move behavior (the Premack principle mentioned earlier) could be used with her in relation to necessary

or satisfying activities. Swimming and tennis could be activities with which she rewards herself *after* she had done some of the things which have become difficult for her, such as shopping, cooking, and helping her husband in the bookshop. I would have her keep a record also of the frequency of her thoughts and feelings about her sister as she goes through a day. How often does it happen? You could ask her to note circumstances that help her go shopping or impede her going shopping, help her do the cooking or impede it, help her assist her husband in their shop or impede that, for further study during interviews, to plan changes in the treatment program. You could ask her to keep notes of any circumstances, events or thoughts just before she has thoughts and feelings about her sister (as when she passes those paintings in the hall).

Having taken note of the kinds of observations I have mentioned, during this first interview, you need also to decide what to do over the next one or two days. Once you have decided that her life is not at risk, you are, of course, much freer than if you decide her life is at risk. I would be inclined to say, "I had better see you in a day or two," for a review of the things that she and I had agreed to make note of or to count, and for possible graphing on a behavior chart, if she likes. Some people turn out, much to your surprise, to love making graphs, when you might have thought that they had no familiarity with a graph and needed a course in elementary algebra.

Suppose the first interview is now over. What might the next steps be in a therapist's program with such a patient? Her log would inform the therapist of circumstances which would increase her coping ability or decrease it. New interventions could be planned to help her move in the direction that she desires (not that I desire). Her log would inform the therapist of the frequency of thoughts and feelings about the sister or circumstances which favor the occurrence of these thoughts and circumstances which decrease them. Her log would refine and dis-

criminate the various thoughts and feelings about the sister because of the inclusion of anecdotal information. All of the welter
of feelings that she described in the videotaped interview will
begin to separate out so that you can focus on one at a time,
perhaps. New interventions could be planned to deal with the
more specifically identified thoughts and feelings.

Particularly in relation to the patient's thoughts and feelings
about her sister, I would use the procedures mentioned earlier
by Jerome Frank, which he called "implosion." I have not used
that term for it. I really have not found a good term for what
it is that I do here, and it is not covered by the behavior therapy framework or any learning theory at the present time. I
use a variety of procedures which include guided fantasy (for
example, I would encourage her to live through a conversation
with her sister, after she had killed herself, if she feels she is
doomed to follow her sister). I would instruct her to have a
guided fantasy which could play an important role in getting
her to keep coping with this and other concerns. Or I might
encourage her to practice what I have described as self-confrontation—to spend a limited period of time, usually not more than
five minutes, as many times a day as necessary, starting it herself, stopping it herself. During those five minutes, she attempts
to relive as vividly as possible in her imagination a particular problem, such as the incomprehensibility of the sister's
behavior; to include every thought she had about it, notice her
feelings while she was having these thoughts, describe the situations, speak out loud if possible. This means she has to be alone
in order not to be humiliated or embarrassed. She notices her
bodily sensations while she is going through this experience.
Then she stops at the end of five minutes and observes what
happens next.

Such self-confrontation or guided fantasy could be practiced
with reference to many of her behavioral features that I mentioned as being available in the interview. "I feel I have to fol-

low her" is a theme which could be made the subject of a guided fantasy or self-confrontation. "It's all such an enigma" could be a separate theme or be a subject of interview interaction. "She made me feel so dependent, so inadequate" could be a theme to work on with self-confrontations. You could use for self-confrontation, "the way in which sister Jean used to make me feel uncomfortable," or "the way in which she did not seem to be a real person because of her actress role and behavior." You could use, for such a procedure, a visit to her apartment and "sharing the possessions she willed to me, the furniture and the car, with my brothers." The patient could make the three paintings at the end of the hall the subject of self-confrontation or guided fantasy. She could do the same with her difficulties with her grandson, which were left completely undefined in the interview material we have, and with her situation involving the unemployed daughter.

A last question about subsequent work with her is, "Who else might be included?" Obviously, you would want to know something about how the husband sees all this, what her relation is with her husband. The therapist will have to decide when he would like the husband to come with her. You would like to have her consent to see the husband as well as the daughter so as to observe the pattern of their interactions with the patient.

What else might be included? The therapist must decide whether to use antidepressant drugs or consider electroshock therapy. If he did not have enough information to make him worry about her immediate safety, he might leave as brief an interval as possible before he sees her again. If he were worried about her safety, but still preferred to hold off electroshock or anti-depressant drugs, he might insist that she accept her husband's being with her for the next 24 or so hours until the next appointment.

In many settings, where there is no physician available who

can write prescriptions or administer E.C.T., problems just as serious as these can be handled by frequent interactional support by the therapist.

The application of some of the above mentioned principles to situations that are common and often far more troublesome to resolve by other means is illustrated in the case of a 24-year-old man who was recovering from injuries in an auto accident. His injuries appeared to be healing steadily, and he was on a prescribed pain medication schedule, but the staff noticed an increasing frequency of requests or demands for pain medication in between the scheduled times. His associated behavior and talk suggested that he might not require the pain medication and that progressive drug dependence might develop if the requests continued to be granted, or if he were permitted to take medication whenever he felt the need for it.

Three procedures were decided on by the staff:

1. The regular pain medication schedule would continue.

2. The nurse responsible for his care would initiate conversation on any one of a variety of topics that might interest him, excluding the topic of pain. She would respond to and try to continue any non-pain topic initiated by the patient.

3. The nurse would ignore, as tactfully and unobtrusively as she could, any requests for pain medication outside the scheduled pain medications.

A graph of non-pain topics per period of nurse-patient contact sampled on four separate days over a two-week period revealed a frequency change from 0 to 15 per day.

A graph of the requests for pain medication during the same periods revealed a change from 5 to 0 per day.

The vertical axis is a log scale that allows a wide range of frequencies of behaviors to be recorded, from one behavior in a day to 1000 in a minute; the horizontal axis is in days, and allows for 140 days of consecutive observations.

The principles illustrated here are (1) the decrease in frequency of an undesired, worrisome or distressing behavior while there is an increase in the frequency of a social and acceptable behavior already within the person's repertoire of abilities; (2) the greater ease of increasing desired, effective, acceptable behaviors than of decreasing undesired behaviors; (3) the quick, dramatic, documented outcome of interventions that are keyed directly to identified behavioral features; (4) the persistence of the desired outcome after the intervention is over.

A 20-year-old woman in a two-bed patient unit wanted to know well ahead of time exactly what diagnostic, examination and treatment procedures would be administered. She made her wishes known by shouting them at the staff, or else she shouted at the staff if she was unprepared for some event involving her.

The staff made four decisions:

1. To obtain a baseline record of the frequency of her shouting at staff during a specified period, before any intervention program was started.

2. After the baseline record was obtained, to initiate brief conversations with her several times each day, designed to inform her of and to explain scheduled or anticipated doctor and nurse procedures, as well as other hospital routines, that affected her, and to elicit her own questions about upcoming events that day. This procedure was to be followed during stated nurse on-duty times.

3. Nurse on duty to remain neutral during shouting behavior.

4. To cease the intervention program after changed behavior was documented, and to continue the daily recording of the frequency of the shouting behavior for a period thereafter.

These four decisions resulted in a reduction of frequency of undesired behavior from a high of ten shouts per hour to none per hour—a reduction produced not by direct attempts to stop the behavior but as an indirect consequence of the staff's increasing the frequency and duration of desirable and acceptable behaviors of their own keyed to her identified concerns and within her repertoire of responsive capabilities. As is not uncommon, the new behavioral pattern, if desirable, effective, and reinforced, outlasts the planned intervention (frequency counts after the intervention ranged from two to zero per hour).

The approach I have presented differs from the notion of "behavior modification," as a highly limited, coercive procedure. Simple procedures of the kind I have described have been documented as having successful, relatively speedy outcomes. New procedures of this kind are being published regularly in several journals. They are compatible with the use of other basic clinical, interpersonal and psychotherapeutic skills. Therapists can learn with whom they are appropriate, and when in therapy they are appropriate.

6

Group Therapies

Morton A. Lieberman, Ph.D.

The Patient

A scant ten years ago, the issue provided by the patient we have observed through the videotape would have provided an easy framework for discussion. The depressed 60-year-old woman entering the portals of the mental health clinic would automatically have set off a number of thoughts, including the appropriateness or inappropriateness of the use of groups for treating the particular psychological misery of such a patient. Most of us who practice group therapy would probably have raised a number of questions about the unique opportunities and pitfalls of a group for such a patient.

Would she be able to tolerate the relatively lengthy period necessary in a traditional psychotherapeutic group before the setting became a viable, manageable environment and before the attachments among members—which in many ways function in lieu of positive transference—could develop, or would such a patient so desperately need prompt relief that she

---

** Portions of this paper are adaptations from People Changing Groups: The New and Not So New, *The American Handbook of Psychiatry*, S. Arieti, Ed., Vol. IV, Basic Books. In press.

would be likely to flee from the group? Given her history, could she cope with the frequent rivalry so characteristic of the group at its early stages and would she be able to share the attention of a therapist? More importantly, could she come to invest in the others in the group so that the relationships she experienced with relative strangers could become significant as a vehicle for exploration? Would the unique features of a group setting, such as its opportunity for members to discover that they are not alone in their misery or that, more often than not, typical defense and coping strategies are bypassed by an emotional contagion which causes patients to experience ego-alien feelings and thoughts, have made this a viable or counter-productive treatment setting for the patient? To what extent would the unique opportunities of a group for social comparison and feedback from peers suit such a patient? To what extent would the opportunities afforded in a group for sense of belonging and communion help her? Would a supportive environment that encourages experimentation with new forms of behavior be central in her therapy?

My own sense is that the patient's deep ambivalence about treatment and her effort to close up and deny would make her an unlikely candidate for group psychotherapy. The findings of a number of investigators which suggest the functional appropriateness of denial mechanisms in older persons would discourage me from immediately seeking to place the patient in a group. Some themes in her life would suggest that useful work could be done in a group context, but most likely one would like to explore brief psychotherapeutic contact to determine the degree to which work with the immediate crisis would be sufficient for such a patient. It would only be later on, if more work were needed, that a group could be considered.

Strictly speaking, a group therapist would have needed to act purely on clinical judgment. The empirical base for choosing the treatment modality, particularly group versus individual psychotherapy, provides scant evidence for a rational decision. By and large, our knowledge in this area is primitive and the existing studies would have provided only rough guides for exclusion, but not inclusion, principles. Over three-quarters of the patients entering a traditional psychothera-peutically-oriented clinic are probably equally suited for group or individual dynamically-oriented therapies. As unfortunately is so often true in our profession, we probably can do a much better job of predicting failures than of selecting those who would do better under one mode of treatment than another.

But for me, the dilemma that faces professionals now, rather than the neat decision-making process of 10 years ago, is the real question of whether it might be more likely that such a person would present himself to the clinic, rather than to the many other settings which offer activities directed toward aiding individuals with their psychological problems. By and large, these activities take place within the group context.

The Current Uses of Small Groups for Healing

Thus, my intention is to offer an overview of the current uses of small groups for healing—what they are, their origins, and their possible future. Much of my attention will be devoted to group-organized mental health activities that may appear to lie outside the boundaries of group therapy, because distinc-tions between group psychotherapies and other uses of groups for healing are increasingly difficult to make. We have been accustomed to think of such distinctions in terms of differences in the clients served, an assumption that, as I hope to demon-strate, is unwarranted. Others make such distinctions on the grounds that group therapy is the province of professionals, whereas the wide variety of other types of healing groups com-monly are led by laymen. Increasingly, this distinction becomes hard to maintain. One can find well-credentialed professionals practicing the range from traditional to "wild man" forms of group healing efforts. Those who lead today's people-changing groups outside of traditional settings are often professionals who have been prepared by long years of training in prestigious institutions; but leaders are also often individuals whose preparation has consisted of no more than a two-week institute or, for that matter, no more than a purely personal judgment that they have something to give.

The blurring of boundary lines between the more traditional healing groups and their modern counterparts is further exacerbated by the increasing variation in the institutional settings in which group healing activities take place. While many healing groups are still to be found in traditional help-giving settings, more and more frequently such activities are conducted in growth centers—a new institution specifically formed for conducting people-changing groups—in church basements, dormitories, living rooms. For good or ill, innovations in recent years have largely emanated, not from traditional mental health professionals, but from the newer forms of group activity. The new group forms are increasingly affecting the practice of group psychotherapy, a fact which increases the difficulty of distinguishing the professionally dominated forms from the newer, more non-professional forms. Finally, it is clear that the newer forms of group healing are serving the largest mass of clients who come seeking relief from psychological stress.

A Brief History

The use of groups for systematically helping individuals in distress is of relatively recent origin in modern mental health practice. It is perhaps helpful to recall, however, that small groups have always served as important healing agents. From the beginning of recorded history, group forces have been used to inspire hope, increase morale, offer strong emotional support, induce a sense of serenity and confidence in the bene-volence of the universe, and so on, so serving to counteract many psychic and bodily ills. Religious healers have always relied heavily on group forces, but when healing passed from the priestly to the medical profession, the conscious use of group forces fell into a decline concomitant with the increasing sanctity of the doctor-patient relationship.

The strangeness experienced by many seekers of psychiatric help, when confronted with the help-giving conditions of groups, is the result of a complex process affecting both those who seek the help as well as those who give it. The devel-opment of psychiatry as an entrenched part of modern medicine was in part predicated on the idea that "scientific medicine" must at all costs distinguish itself from healing which stemmed from nonscientific traditions. Modern Western psychiatry was even more plagued than other branches of medicine with the need to become "scientific." In its beginnings, the medical treatment of psychological problems required for its legitimiza-tion as a branch of medical science a clear differentiation be-tween its methods and those that preceded it in non-Western societies, where highly developed group-based techniques were used for curing psychological illness within the framework of the family, the group of similar sufferers, the village, or the religious community. This association of "pre-scientific" thera-pies with group forms perhaps influenced psychiatry away from utilization of group techniques.

In Western culture, it has been expected that personal help would be given by one person—it could be the corner bar-tender, a personal friend, or a professional, such as a lawyer, doctor, or clergyman—but what is important is that it has been expected that it would be rendered in an intimate, private, and exclusive context. Even in such bodies as the family or the church, it was until recently generally assumed that personal help would be offered and received in a private, two-person relationship, not through the group as a whole. The historical roots of modern psychiatry and the general Western cultural context of the first half of the twentieth century did not create conditions suitable for the flourishing growth of group-based healing technologies.

Still, the often competing concepts of individual psychotherapy have, oddly enough, been the main source of theory underlying various forms of group treatment in current use, a fact which goes far to explain why the degree of conceptual morass in contemporary theorizing about group treatment practice is as broad as the degree of disagreement regarding principles of individual psychotherapy. Most major schools of psychotherapy have generated their counterpart in group psychotherapy. More often than not the counterparts of dyadically-generated theories of psychotherapy have had a haphazard growth pattern developed more out of necessity and accident than out of systematic theoretical explanation. Individuals trained in a particular school of therapy conduct groups based on tenets derived from their particular orientation to individual therapy. Often techniques and concepts have been adapted to the multi-person situation with little formal thought given to the consequences that may be generated by the addition of multi-person social forces to the treatment context.

The so-called "new therapies" share a similar history. Although some of the newer ideas were generated out of a movement away from a psychoanalytic view of pathology toward more humanistic or existential theories of personality, the old and the new are similar in that they stem from theories of individual psychotherapy, not from concepts regarding the influence of the group on processes of individual change. Thus, despite a rich largesse of technique and a tenuous commitment to their pragmatic beginnings, both "new" and "old" group treatment forms share a common ailment—an inappropriate, and consequently barren and confusing, conceptual base. The dyadically-oriented intellectual battles over the competing ideas offered up by various systems of individual psychotherapy are reenacted in the new group arenas without even a pause to ask whether the concepts being questioned have any relevance to groups.

Before proceeding to examine the various systems of people-changing that occur in groups, it is useful to provide some sense data on what these activities look like. Let me try to draw composite pictures of both psychotherapy as it has commonly been practiced within traditional mental health settings and some of the "newer therapies."

An Illustration—The New and Not So New

To observe the initial session of a traditional group therapy session, for example, would be to experience something like this:

About nine people file into a room slowly, tentatively. Each has previously seen only one other person in the room—the therapist, a week earlier, in a diagnostic interview. Some appear reluctant, some enthusiastic, but all have come to this first meeting with at least the willingness to go along with the therapist's belief that the group could be useful to them. They sit in a circle, quiet and expectant. Their posture seems anxious. What will go on here? What can go on here? What will the therapist do? Several in the group have had previous psychotherapy. One woman begins the interaction by describing the disappointments she has experienced in previous treatments. A note of desperation and near panic is discernible in the responses of others to her wail of self-negation and helplessness. Sympathetic offerings of similar tales of woe are heard from various people in the room. From time to time the therapist comments, pointing out the fearful expectations of the various group members.

Underneath the "stories" and histories offered by various members, the therapist "hears" the patients asking each other a set of questions only hinted at in what they are saying. And underneath the questions about others in the room lies still another set, all having to do with the person himself. Why did you come? What are your hopes? What forms does your "illness" take? Do you feel that this may do me any good at all? Are you as sick as I? Am I as sick as you? How strange, perhaps even insane, is the arrangement whereby I come to a group of neurotics to get better. Above all, what is the "doctor" over there planning to do for me? I don't like people—why must I be here? Who are these others and what have I to do with them?

Thus, group therapy begins. The patients begin an experience in treatment which they may understandably feel violates expectations they bring from their experience in other doctor-patient relationships. Often group therapy patients cannot see what good it will do an unhappy neurotic person to share his "problems" with other neurotic sufferers. Is it enough to reassure him, as some therapists indeed believe, that a "problem shared is a problem helped" or to provide a context founded on the assumption that misery not only loves but is relieved by company? What of the therapist? Will he, by virtue of some rare professional training and intuitive attributes, be able to understand, diagnose, and change the troublesome personality patterns of a lifetime? And of a roomful of people simultaneously? He—the therapist—obviously expects something useful to come from the interactions of these people, but how does he see the members to be of use to each other when he remains silent and passive so long? What does he expect will happen?

At the other end of the group treatment continuum we can imagine another group of people temporarily migrating to a growth center. Their arrival is noisier, more buoyant, more playful; they are robed in vacation garb, their talk is free and more reminiscent of the first evening at summer camp than the still, anxious scene of the group therapy session. They are likely to have a speaking knowledge of Maslow, Rogers, Berne, and Perls, and of the latest people-changing procedures. They freely express their desire for change and seem eager to get to know one another. They seem hardly able to await the morning's beginning; if some appear a bit anxious, others are enthusiastic about the drama that will unfold. All know in general what they can expect to happen, but seem restless to generate the specific emotions and events which will form the content of their shared experience.

What will the leader, whom they have never met, be like? What will he do or expect of them? In the back of their minds is the accumulation of images based on what they have heard from friends and the popular press—images which are mixed with desires to become changed people. Will it work for me? What about the others? Will they really get to know me? Can I trust them? Will they help me?

They do not have long to wait; the leader begins with an explosion of his inner feelings. He may be sleepy this morning, he may not have wanted to come, he may look around and find the group full of "unattractive people" and "tell it like it is" without pausing. On the other hand, he may express his total positive regard for all and quickly exhibit a readiness to accept any behavior expressed. He may then launch into a set of instructions, perhaps suggesting that "all of you look so 'up tight' that we ought to loosen up and begin by playing a childhood game."

The images evoked by these two settings are intended to suggest that the group-based people-changing business in our society today has diverse assumptions, allegiances, and expectations, to the point that it might appear sheer folly to consider them under the same rubric.

Comparisons among Healing Groups

A scanning of the field of group-based activities whose central task is the psychological and behavioral alteration of individuals and the relief of human misery would suggest that the range of such activities might be grouped into four major categories. At one end of a continuum would be those activities that formally fall within the purview of societally sanctioned, professionally led groups—group psychotherapy. Group therapy has as its avowed public goal the production of mental health and sees as its relevant population those who define themselves as patients experiencing psychological misery. The activities of group therapy operate explicitly within a medical framework. There is emphasis on malfunctioning, defined in terms of "sick behavior," which the client brings into the formally defined system. One implication of this emphasis is that there are individuals within society who would be legitimized as appropriate patients, and those who would be seen as inappropriate.

At the opposite end of the professional continuum are a variety of self-help movements: Alcoholics Anonymous, Synanon, Recovery Inc., etc., up to perhaps as many as 216 separate organizations. By intention these groups are not professionally led. As lay movements, however, they share some notions of appropriate clientele with group psychotherapy. The definition of appropriate clientele is usually much narrower than in group psychotherapy, but there are clear-cut inclusion-exclusion principles. One must be an alcoholic, an abuser of drugs, a child-abuser, a parent of a child who has a particular disease, and so forth. The range for any particular self-help movement's attention is limited to individuals who have a common symptom, problem or life predicament.

A third set of healing groups comes under the rubric of the Human Potential Movement, including such variously labeled activities as sensitivity training, encounter groups, and so on. Although there are many instances of non-professional leaders, these activities usually do involve professionals, whether legitimized by traditional psychological and psychiatric disciplines or by newer types of training institutions. A major distinction between the previously mentioned activities and encounter or growth groups is that the latter view themselves as having universal applicability. Unlike group therapy which emphasizes patienthood, or self-help programs which emphasize a common problem, the encounter movement emphasizes that its activities are relevant to all who want to change, grow, and develop.

Finally, we come to consciousness-raising groups, which share with self-help groups the non-professional orientation and peer control, but, unlike the self-help groups, have broad criteria for inclusion. Although they do not take in everyone, as does the Human Potential Movement, consciousness-raising groups are formed on the basis of certain general demographic similarities: sex, race, ethnicity, age, or sexual behavior. The tie that binds is not a common syndrome but a general characteristic of a large subgroup of people, and permits wide latitude regarding personal particularities.

Although all of these activities are taking place in groups, is it reasonable to assume that they are serving similar functions as alternatives to traditional mental health systems? Are such groups the relevant concern of psychiatry? The question can be answered in several ways. The issue of just what is a relevant concern of psychiatry is heavily value-laden. There are many who believe that the only legitimate concerns of psychiatry are the mental illnesses. I feel neither competent to address this issue, nor do I believe it appropriate but will sidestep it by noting that much of current practice of mental health does concern itself with a broad range of troubled individuals who come to us occasionally with classical neurotic problems, perhaps more and more frequently with problems that we label "existential concerns," and certainly with concerns about various unhappinesses or disturbances in their interpersonal world. If we look at such people, I can offer some evidence that at least one such institution-using, group-based change system outside of traditional psychotherapy attracts people who are in many ways similar to patients who enter formal or traditional mental health systems.

A Study of Growth Center Participants

During the past decade, a new form of institution, the growth center, has spread across the United States, as well as other Western societies. A major theme of this new institution has been to move away from defining people who need psychological help as "patients." Yet, some recently developed information suggests that perhaps the newer forms which emphasize growth and the development of human potential may not be attracting a different population from that engaged in psychotherapy (1). This study provides survey information on the users of these new activities: Why do they come? What do they expect? How, if at all, do they differ from the users of traditional psychotherapy? Specifically, do the goals and the expectations of patients entering traditional mental health institutions differ from the goals and expectations of participants who enter activities in the Human Potential Movement?

Self-administered questionnaires were sent out to 656 prospective participants at five growth centers. A contrast sample was generated from similar questionnaires given to 150 applicants to five private psychiatric clinics. The questionnaires for both samples were completed prior to participation in activities at the growth centers or clinics. Return rates of 65% for the growth centers and 59% for the clinics brought the final sample size to 426 growth center participants and 89 psychotherapy patients.

A broad range of questions about motivations, perceptions, and attitudes was asked. Two measures of psychological disturbance were included which, in previous studies, differentiated psychiatric patients from non-patients: Life Stress (2) and (self-reported) Psychiatric Symptoms (3). Assessments were also made in the following areas: motivational, such as help seeking, educational, social, recreational; attitudes towards, and perceptions of, growth center leaders (or therapists) in terms of authority, egalitarianism, and expertise; time orientations; amount of expected change; and images of growth centers and psychotherapy in terms of their participants, process, and outcome.

The growth center population was examined for its help-seeking characteristics. A national probability sample provided normative data on stress and symptoms for contrasts with the clinic and growth center samples.

Growth center participants had significantly higher stress (p<.001) and symptoms scores (p<.0001) than did the normative population. Social class and age were statistically controlled. Help seeking was widely endorsed as a motive for attending such centers, and 81% of the prospective participants had either been or were currently in psychotherapy. Thus, the "patient-like" characteristics of those attending growth centers emerged strongly on all the variables examined and the phrase "therapy for normals" would not characterize most of the sample. They resemble a clinic population much more than they do a normal population. Nor do the data support a hypothesis that growth centers are an alternative pathway for help getting. Most applicants are currently experiencing distress in their lives and have sought outside help with it, both in psychotherapy and from growth center groups. They seem not so much to have chosen one over the other as to have chosen both.

The myth that the Human Potential Movement appeals to

hedonistic, playful seekers after joy is not borne out by the data. Rather, their goals are instrumental and focus primarily around issues of obtaining help with personal problems. For half to three-quarters of the sample, participants' stated reasons for attending include bringing about change in themselves, dealing with current life problems, improving their relationships with people, solving long-term personal hang-ups, becoming a new person, seeking increased meaning in life, expanding their consciousness, and increasing their self-awareness and body-awareness. Only a handful come for a vacation, to get away, to turn on, to have intense emotional experiences, or to seek new sexual experiences. Nor do they seek primarily to cope with alienation. Few come to meet people, find community, or relieve feelings of loneliness.

The appeal of the growth center's egalitarian qualities—the diminished status and power differentials between client and leader in contrast to the supposedly more authoritarian relationship which exists between patient and therapist—has frequently been cited as a reason for the rising popularity of the centers. Our data do not support such a distinction, however. There are no differences between the samples in their perceptions of leaders' (or therapists') special power or expertise. Furthermore, those who enter growth centers with the avowed purpose of relieving their distress do, more than all other groups including therapy patients, seek expert help when faced with interpersonal problems. There is little evidence, then, to suggest that growth center goers represent a unique population of egalitarian-oriented individuals who have rejected the traditional structures of society for getting help. Despite the existential rhetoric of the human potential movement, those who seek out these activities are instrumentally rather than existentially oriented. They believe that technologies exist for solving all human problems.

Participants in growth center activities, compared to therapy patients, place more emphasis on the present than the future and on immediate rather than delayed gratification. They feel that present joys are more important than a distant good and are not willing to endorse the position that present sacrifices lead to future rewards. When one looks at their actual expectations for change over time, however, they are not wildly optimistic. Their time span is somewhat shorter, so that growth center participants expect to make significantly more progress by the end of one month than therapy patients expect. However, this difference disappears in ratings of progress by six months, and by one year it is the psychotherapy patients who expect to make more progress toward their goals. Thus, the adherence to an existential "live for today" ethic is more rhetoric than reality and the myth that growth centers appeal to the miracle seekers is not supported by the findings.

The strongest differences between therapy patients and growth center participants were found in their respective views of the process by which change occurs. Growth center participants expected, much more than did therapy patients, to experience feelings of excitement and joy and to experiment with new forms of behavior by doing and saying things they had not previously done.

The particular form of growth center activity these participants attended seems to have had little to do with their motivation for entering—whether their "thing" is a Gestalt encounter, a week of meditation, a course in biofeedback, or any of the other widely-ranging, people-changing activities offered in a typical growth center. In some subsequent work based on depth interviews, two important themes emerged. Those who have selected themselves to be participants in such settings, as compared with more traditional patients, have an orientation to change which implies the absence of pain in the change process. Those who attend growth centers do form a unique subculture in our society—they are attuned, in almost a life-style way, to reliance on institutional structures for helping them with interpersonal and personal problems. In this sense, they are much more dependent upon institutional structures for resolving their psychological misery than are the general population and even those who enter traditional mental health systems. Typically, they have spent long years moving from one form of institutional change or therapy to another; it is a repetitive pattern on which life is focused almost as if they have little belief that they will find solace, but are committed to the process of looking.

If both the goals and the client systems overlap among the various settings that use group methods for healing, what are some of the important distinctions among them? In making judgments about the various systems, especially with regard to appropriateness for a particular individual, it is helpful to consider the following comparison.

Structural and Technical Differences among Groups

Perhaps the most important technological change characterizing the newer forms is reflected in techniques for *lessening the psychological distance* between leader and participant. A variety of methods serve this function; the transparency of the therapist (personal revelations and so forth), the use of warm informal settings, the emphasis on assuming the stance of participant, the emphasis that characterizes some of the new forms on diminishing the importance of expertise of the leader and defining him more nearly as a peer and, finally, the use of physical contact—touching—are all devices which seem calculated to reduce the psychological distance between the changer and the changing.

Few guides exist to assess the importance of such a change from the traditional patient-therapist relationship. Perhaps all that can be said for certain is that it reflects current changes in social mores, which have increasingly moved away from emphasis on the priestly status of healing professionals and other experts. The new forms could be said to be more sensitive than the old to current cultural expectations.

A second major distinction between therapy and encounter groups, on the one hand, and most self-help and consciousness-raising groups, on the other, relates to their conception of the function of the group as a mechanism for personal change. Both psychotherapy and encounter groups of almost all theoretical persuasions share, as a fundamental assumption, a view of the group as a *social microcosm*. It is this aspect of the group—its reflection of the interpersonal issues that confront individuals in the larger society—that is most highly prized as the group property which induces individual change. Varying types of encounter and psychotherapeutic schools of thought differ, of course, over which transactions are most important—those between patient and therapist or those among patients. They also differ regarding which emotional states are most conducive to positive change. But underneath all the activities that fall into these two types lies the assumption that cure or change is based on the exploration and reworking of relationships in the group.

Self-help groups and consciousness-raising groups develop a rather different stance on the issue of the group as a microcosm. The interaction among members as a vehicle for change appears to be somewhat de-emphasized. The group is a supportive environment for developing new behavior not within the group primarily, but outside. The group becomes a vehicle for cognitive restructuring, but analysis of the transactions among members is not the basic tool of change.

Another characteristic that contrasts these four systems is the degree to which they stress *differentiation* versus nondifferentiation among their members. Belonging to the vague class of "being neurotic," or having psychological difficulty, or being a patient, is a vague and relatively unbound identification compared to being a member of a minority group—for example, a woman in a consciousness-raising group. Being interested in growth and development is indistinct, and is obviously a more obscure basis for forming an identity with a communal effort than being an alcoholic or a child abuser. It is easier in consciousness-raising groups and self-help groups to stress identity with a common core problem than it is in psychotherapy and other groups. Although it is typical for a psychotherapeutic group to go through a period of time in which similarities are stressed, this is usually an early developmental phase, and represents an attempt of the group to achieve some form of cohesiveness. It is not the *raison d'être* of the group, as it may be for a consciousness-raising or self-help group. In fact, we have some evidence that individuals who remain committed in encounter groups to a sense of similarity are less likely to be changed positively by such an experience (4). However, the potency of both the self-help groups and the consciousness-raising groups appears to stem from their continued insistence on the possession of a common problem and members believe they derive support from their identification with a common core issue.

An obvious distinction among the various systems of group-based healing rests in their *attribution system*—the cognitive and conative structure explicitly and implicitly communicated regarding the source of human misery and how one resolves it. An obvious example would be the degree to which the systems emphasize internal versus external sources of the problem. We are all familiar with psychotherapeutic systems that attribute the source of psychological difficulty to the personal past. Contrast this with the women's consciousness-raising movement, which emphasizes an external locus of the problem: an impersonal, sexist society. In our attempt to understand what processes may be psychotherapeutic, we have paid too little attention to the effect of varying attribution systems on change. One of the intriguing impressions we had from our study of encounter groups (4), in comparing a wide variety of theories of change as expressed in leader orientation, was that it did not seem to make much difference which theory was "taught" as long as some cognitive structure was gained from the group to explain one's problems and how to resolve them. Whether this observation would fit the larger differences in attribution systems one can assume between, for example, a psychotherapeutic group and a women's consciousness-raising group is a major unknown.

The last issue I'd like to examine is the role of the therapist or group leader in people-changing groups. Here I would like to shift our emphases from examining the range of systems to focusing on those two systems that involve formally legitimized leaders—group psychotherapy and encounter groups.

Therapists' Contributions to Therapeutics

Theories of personal change in groups usually give great emphasis to concepts addressed to the relationship of the leader to the patients. Similar to theories of individual therapy, they emphasize the central importance of the therapist. It is through his actions or abstinence from action that change processes are initiated and are set in the right (or the wrong) direction. Theories are maximally distinguishable by the particular dimensions of the leader/client relationship they emphasize. For some, the core concepts relate to the interpersonal conditions the leader creates between himself and each participant—positive regard, genuineness, and so forth. Others stress the leader's symbolic properties, such as the specific transference relationship between each patient and the leader, while others stress the symbolic relationship of the leader to the *group as a whole*. Still others, although also stressing the unique relationship of each patient to the leader, emphasize negative rather than positive interaction through such devices as the "hot seat," in which the group acts as Greek chorus or background to this primary relationship.

Despite such fundamentally different conclusions about what the crucial leader "inputs" are, however, all these theories agree on the centrality of the leader to the change process; it is he who sets up the learning experience, who makes the interpretations or analyses resistance, who sets up the norms, who is the "model," and so forth. The specific content of the leader's actions and responsibilities may differ, but the underlying assumption is that the central factor in changing people is what the leader does or how he expresses himself.

It is possible, however, that the behavior, personality, and skill level of the leader has taken on mythic proportions as a basic causal force explaining successful personal change in groups. Some obvious factors in the history and development of groups for people changing may have contributed to this view. Theories of group change of individuals naturally have given great prominence to the role of the leader—after all, most of these theories have arisen from leaders who have often also been highly charismatic individuals. It is understandable that the clinicians who have developed what little theory there is on changing people through groups might be somewhat myopic and could easily be pardoned if they have overestimated the contribution of the leader (i.e., themselves) to the curative process. No theories of group personal change are broadly accepted that have developed out of the thinking of the patients or out of experimental psychology, with the possible exception of some applications of behavioral modification theory that are used in group contexts. Thus, the assumption of leader centrality found in most theories of group personal change may represent an understandable overestimation on the part of the theorists based on their unique perspective of the process about which they attempt to theorize.

But what about transference? Could anyone who has ever worked with a people-changing group realistically ignore the magical expectations, distortions, overestimations, that are directed toward the person of the leader? No matter what one labels the feelings and thoughts of members toward their leader, it is hard to ignore transference as a central phenomenon common to all people-changing groups. I see no reason to doubt that the complex, convoluted, supercharged feelings that focus on the person of the therapist do exist. Many would agree that the leader need not do anything more than be there to become enhanced with the aura of a professional—a person capable of giving help, of performing a priestly function.

Whether or not transference is a universal product of psychotherapeutic contact, however, the fact of transference reactions where indeed they do occur does not, in and of itself, *demonstrate* that the leader is central to the curative process. That supercharged feelings toward the leader are usually generated in a group context does not permit one to jump to the conclusion that transference is intrinsically a curative factor in the group context. In other words, no unquestionable cause-effect relationship relative to outcome is demonstrated merely by the evidence that leaders usually become objects of transference.

In addition to the observation that most theories of group personal change have grown out of the experience of leaders or therapists themselves, and that the virtual omnipresence of transference has been taken as proof that the leader is central, several other conditions may be observed which may "account for" the strong belief that the leader is central. Professionalization, the length of time invested in training, the sharp boundaries surrounding the help-giving professions, the distinctive languages, the fee structures, etc. are all conditions that would imply the "helpfulness" of considering the leader to be central, prominent, critical in the curative process. It seems reasonable to think that, to the degree that an activity in our society becomes professionalized, so will the role of the professional who conducts the activity become enhanced in the minds of both the professional and the layman. Consider for a moment the full implications of discovering that most of what helps patients in groups stems from the relationships members have to one another and to processes that are only tangentially related to the behavior and person of the leader. Such a view would in all certainty present difficulties for continued dismissal of questions regarding whether professionalization is necessary, or how much.

It is natural that theories of group personal change, as a latter day development, should have been influenced by images of the obvious influence and control leaders exercise in dyadic therapy. This historical fact probably accounts, to some extent, for the prevalent assumption that the person and behavior of the leader are critical in group personal change.

Thus, many forces exist for creating a mythology surrounding the person of the leader. Journals and professional meetings endlessly encourage debates which support the "prominence" of the therapist or leader through discussions of what he does, how he does it, when he does it, how he feels, what his hangups are, how aware he is, what his theory is, whether he works alone or with a co-therapist, whether "he" is he or she, black or white, kindly or hostile, and so on.

What data, then, can the field bring to bear on this issue—not whether groups help people, but whether what the therapist or leader does is central in that help-giving process and, if not, what precisely can be specified as essential leader inputs?

The empirical findings available in the literature offer only a few crumbs, and cannot provide evidence for a reasoned position on the question of how much the therapist or leader contributes to the outcome of patients. Some perspective on the

question is offered via the analogy from individual psychotherapy relative to the non-specific treatment or placebo effects. For
the groups, the analogues to placebo effects are certain events
that frequently occur in small face-to-face intensive groups that
can provide experiences which *in themselves* are curative. Because these events coincide with the presence of a leader—
and one often perceived as in possession of magical qualities—
their curative power is attributed to the leader.

The data available serve only to legitimize raising this question, they are insufficient to answer it. Studies reporting no
differences in the effectiveness of naive therapists compared to
experienced professionals could be interpreted to mean that the
group situation within rather broad limits is useful regardless of
the specific behavior of the therapist. Studies in which large
outcome differences were found among experienced therapists
might, on the other hand, suggest an alternative conclusion—
that the behaviors of the therapist are critical. If we look
closely at these studies, however, an alternate explanation could
be offered. Suppose for a moment we make the assumption that
the major impact of therapists or leaders is to make people
worse. Let us also play with the assumption that there are only
two major factors operating in therapeutic groups—the intrinsic
beneficial effects of the group itself and the inputs of the leader,
most of which are non-beneficial. The notion behind these assumptions is to establish as the appropriate zero point for
assessing the leader contribution not a non-treatment control
situation, but rather a treatment situation minus the leader.

In the encounter group study, 16 groups with leaders who
had 10 or more years of experience in conducting groups were
compared to groups which had no other leader than Berzon's
peer tape program. Of the 16 groups with leaders only four
exceeded the mean score of the two tape groups; the other 12
did worse than the tape groups, some considerably worse. While
the tape groups, of course, were not leaderless in the strict-

est sense, the tape situation offered only a minimal structure to the participants. Thus, it seems reasonable to assume that the tape group creates conditions reflecting the curative power of the group under minimal leader "input" and therefore has implications regarding the constructive potential of a group without the intervention of a professional leader.

Data such as these could, of course, be interpreted, like the data in which naive therapists are compared to expert practitioners, as suggesting that most therapists are relatively incompetent. This has, in fact, been the usual approach to such "disturbing" findings when they appear in the literature. The background and professional esteem of the 16 therapists compared to the tape groups make it hard to argue for such an interpretation. These men were clearly competent in executing practices appropriate to their theories of change, but perhaps they were not competent in using maximally the group's inherent curative powers for benefiting patients. Indeed, it is possible that they may have intervened in such ways as to obstruct these naturally beneficial attributes within the group. Findings such as these raise a more important issue: I believe there are processes within a group that in and of themselves are help-producing, so that to demonstrate that people can get better in groups does not answer the question of just what are the contributions of the group leader to the therapeutic process.

Evidence for the positive effects of intensive small group experiences external to the behavior of the leader comes from an examination of specific "curative mechanisms" and particular psychosocial conditions which often lie outside the direct influence of the leader. Normative characteristics of the group —the informal, often inarticulate and undiscerned, social agreements which regulate the behavior of members—were demonstrated in the encounter study to be strong influences on overall outcome scores, perhaps more important than leader behavior. The findings further suggested that leaders contributed a smaller share to establishing the normative structure than what would be expected. Therapeutic mechanisms such as similarity and "spectator therapy"—the ability of a person to identify with the experiences of another without directly participating in them, or experiences of finding similarity between one's self and another human being—were demonstrated as powerful mechanisms for change, mechanisms which arise more from the intrinsic characteristics of intensive peer group experience than from the behavior of the leader. The role and status of the individual in a group—for example, whether he was a deviant in the group or a central person—were also demonstrated to account for successful outcome more than almost any other elements of the change process.

Findings such as these point to the importance of opening debate on the question of the importance of the leader to the group, an assumption that may have thus far served more to confuse than to elucidate. An appreciation of the intensive positive and negative forces inherent in the social microcosm that is the treatment group is perhaps the single most helpful guide toward developing a realistic picture of both the problems and potentials inherent in using groups for people changing.

The crucial problem as to effective use of groups for changing people is how to capitalize on the potency of the group (its capacity to involve, to commit and to move people emotionally) in such a way that this capacity will not be accepted as in itself a sufficient end-product (a product which in all likelihood has been all that has been gained by many of the millions who have tasted the new group roads to growth). How can we employ the power of groups to involve people, to generate their enthusiasm, to exact their commitment, to move them to deep levels of emotionality so that treatment groups or growth groups or whatever they are called will also serve the purpose of helping to resolve the particular brands of human misery that are driving millions to try them out?

The question then becomes, how can one relate the potency of groups, which provides a basis for other processes to occur that do effect change and which forms the basis of attraction of the group (people will stay and participate and get involved), to the creation of a viable learning environment? It is not enough simply to suggest that the potency of a group is not, itself, an effective change mechanism, and thereby allow oneself to ignore it. If for no other reason, one cannot ignore it because the way people package their troubles today and how they see themselves related to a change-inducing situation do not permit dependence on the mores of traditional therapy, in which forebearance, patience, and inner motivation are stressed. Such expectations of the client do not match "where it's at." It is perhaps an overly-generalized view, but I think one that will become increasingly accurate, that group treatment forms cannot succeed in today's world without meeting, to a sizeable degree, the expectations of the members for a potent, moving, emotionally involved experience.

Many dangers lurk in this domain. If therapists and leaders read potency to mean success of treatment, they will err grievously. If they believe they should direct their major attention to behaviors which stimulate group potency, they will have exciting groups which reward them in a highly personal sense, but they will not fulfill their function—to provide a setting that guarantees growth or change.

REFERENCES

1. GARDNER, J. and LIEBERMAN, M. A. Alternative helping systems: A survey comparison between participants in growth center activities and patients in psychiatric clinics. Presented at the 81st Annual Meeting of the American Psychological Association, Montreal, Canada, August 1973. This study was supported by a grant from the National Institute of Mental Health (1-R01-MH-23,772-01): Principal Investigator Morton A. Lieberman, "The Function of the Human Potential Movement."
2. PAYKEL, E. S. and ULENHUTH, J. Scaling of Life Events. *Archives of General Psychiatry*, 25:340-347, 1971.
3. FRANK, J. D. et al. Why Patients Leave Psychotherapy. *Archives of Neurology and Psychiatry*, 77:283-299, 1957.
4. LIEBERMAN, M. A., YALOM, I. D. and MILES, M. B. *Encounter Groups: First Facts*. New York: Basic Books, 1972.

7

Psychopharmacology in a Psychotherapeutic Setting

Shervert H. Frazier, M.D.

When I viewed the taped interview of this depressed lady by Doctor Muslin, I thought it was an excellent example of an associative anamnestic interview in what must have been a devastating shock to the patient's loss two months prior. She looked depressed. She held her face and head, she twirled her wedding ring, she rearranged her hair, she took off and replaced her glasses. She described loss of interest, but we do not know how much and how recent.

There is further information that one would prefer to have before indicating a specific course of therapy for this patient. We would expect these data might emerge in subsequent interviews in order to evaluate more completely some of the issues regarding onset, prior history and other signs. I will indicate what areas of the history I would prefer to have to evaluate therapeutic plans since it bears directly on an approach to the use of pharmacotherapy.

The patient had premonitions she felt she had to follow. Did she show some of Lindemann's physiological signs of shock due to grief? We do not have an adequate history of her mourning and grief (did she go to the funeral?) in the past two months, nor after her mother's death five years ago, nor after her father's death, nor after the death of her brother when she was 15 years old. She used denial of her loss of her sister by using the present tense ("she's 70 now"), she deplored her lack of intimacy with her sister ("I didn't know her"). She deplored her dependency on her sister, who promised her mother on her deathbed to take care of her younger sister (the patient). She felt abandoned *by* her sister, felt a failure *to* her sister, and we do not know how symbiotic their relationship was. She described this period in time as her "last summer." Her way out was sleeping pills. Several times she confronted the interviewer with questions and was not at all a spineless, withdrawn person. Bristling anger was incipient. We have little information about the men in her life; her father seemed vague, her husband was concerned and it was he who called for the appointment, her grandson is at her home and "I love him to death." We have no family history regarding depression, manias, other affective states, recurrent depressions in this woman, the details of the family constellation, how she felt when her mother was pregnant when the patient was 14 or 15 years old, her present and past medical history, history of responses to other drugs and treatments. We saw her near tears on several occasions. Did she weep and grieve on recent occasions when she had seen other persons?

What vegetative signs do we have in her present state? Is she sleeping or suffering from insomnia, has she lost her appetite, lost weight, is she agitated? Do we need a medical examination? A sleep EEG? Is the depression reactive *only* or are there signs of characterological obsessionality, characterological depression, or is the depression beginning to shift toward the endogenous? What is the present evaluation of the suicidal risk? Does she, at 60 years old, have a chronic medical illness? Have other significant family figures committed or attempted suicide? Has she had recurrent depressions?

The real question is, "Can she bear the painful effect of her illness?" If she cannot, then specific interventions seem to me to be needed.

There are about four other things I would do before thinking about prescribing anti-depressants. I would obtain the details needed as described above; I would try to contact the patient *affectively*, especially in the area of her anger at abandonment, loss, separation; I would attempt to help her "let her sister die"; I would make a contract with her to see her again the next day to obtain some more data and to know more of her feelings; I would try to undercut her feeling of inadequacy, do some "accentuating of the positive" ego building to its actual state. She is a person of some accomplishments—attended a conservatory of music, two marriages, a daughter, worked part-time in the family business. I would meet and enlist her husband as an ally in her support, I would define her capacity for object relations, I would try to assist in an ego syntonic way in her time of crisis, I would work hard to reduce her level of aggression, I would try to instill genuine hope. I would question vigorously her premonitions about her own death and her feelings about rejoining her sister in death. I would enlist her brother to take over part of the legal problems of the sister's estate. I would definitely encourage her getting rid of that old furniture and that old car of her sister's. I would find out how she uses alcohol. I would explain her illness to her as an illness. I would obtain a religious history. In this venture, I would begin a dynamic psychotherapy approach to her crisis and, on a time-limited brief basis, try to uncover grief and mourning feelings, carefully watching whether or not development of vegetative signs occurs.

The presence of vegetative signs constitutes the specific indication for anti-depressant medication. The vegetative signs I am referring to are anorexia, weight loss, insomnia and psycho-motor retardation. If they developed, I would start her on anti-depressant medications, recognizing that above the age of 60 inordinate complications such as strokes, heart attacks, arrhyth-mias and side effects may occur. Since we have no standard of comparison for the effectiveness of various anti-depressant med-ications, I would watch the mood and its changes, especially elevations. I would attempt to have the interactions and mood evaluated within other psychotherapeutic modalities, such as group therapies, behavioral modification therapies, encounter therapies, meditational therapies, or religiously oriented ther-apies, if she were not being seen in dynamic therapy.

If one chooses anti-depressants, the most likely therapeutic choice is one of the tricyclics such as amitriptyline or imipra-mine, starting with a test dose of 25 mg. and raising the dosage gradually, always watching for hypotensive or other side effects. These tricyclics sometimes cause latent delusional material to become manifest, as well as increased agitation in some pa-tients, with increasing fragmentation of thought and behavior. The addition of standard phenothiazines to control such agita-tion is sometimes indicated. I would start with 25 mg. TID and increase by 25 mg. every second or third day until I had reached 125-150 mg. total daily dosage. I would hold there for two to three weeks. I am aware that there are those psychopharmacol-ogists who would raise the dosage higher and faster. The con-sensus of several now seems to be that in this age group the higher dosages are not appreciably more helpful. Higher dosages should always be given in a structured situation where physio-logical complications can be monitored, such as in a day care center, day hospital, night hospital, partial hospital or com-munity mental health center, but not necessarily in a 24-hour hospital.

The mood usually lifts gradually. Faith comes back before people-relatedness returns. Some overly controlling therapists set up superstructured regimens which cause the patient to be unable to reach the goals, feel failure again, and regress, causing a recurrence of depression. If bipolar illness exists, I would treat this depression and then start lithium after a careful lithium workup (liver function tests, thyroid evaluation). If the regimen does not work, I would consider adding methylphenidate if I had used imipramine because Perel has shown constitutional drug reactor types as a theoretical possibility and methylphenidate potentiates the effect of imipramine from 1-38 times. If that did not work, I would consider T_3, T_4, or TSH which, according to Prange and Wybrow, and others, helps greatly in women past 40 years of age, and also helps men, though not as much. We have had a few successes in the treatment of otherwise resistant depressions.

So much for management, now what about theory? The greater the number and variety of treatments for an illness, the less likely any one is definitive or completely effective. Most treatment depends on the training of the person involved. Psychologists do not prescribe drugs. Medical doctors often do. The lack of experience with drugs, secondary to the period of training, makes the decision for many. Competitive schools of thought (psychoanalytic, behavioral, somatic therapies) make the decision for others. Almost all overdetermine the treatment prescribed.

It is confusing to try to understand the biochemistry of neurotransmitters and to make a coherent integration of that with psychodynamic and behavioral knowledge and experience. Psychotherapists explained drugs at first as chemical lobotomies, suppressing symptoms and removing the major tool of dynamic therapy-anxiety. Other psychiatrists facetiously said, "Well, psychiatrists are always trying to get inside their patients and giving drugs is another form of that attempt." Other psychiatrists saw drugs as panaceas and heaven-sent answers to untenable theories that needed to have been discarded yesterday.

The "either" central genetic biochemical neurotransmitter "or" the psychogeneticists set up an exclusiveness and competition which deny the "both/and" approach. Certainly psychotherapy and psychogenesis have material of consequence concerning central neurotransmitters. There is no need for this polarization. Neither drugs, central neurotransmitters, nor psycho-surgery will solve the social problems which contribute to the precipitation and cause of mental distress of much of our population. It is my opinion that the psychotherapeutic setting, of whatever type, and the modality of treatment should be combined with psychopharmacological agents when indicated until definitive cures have been evolved for the major mental illnesses. Cure means total reversal, no further occurrences, and no residue. We are dealing with multiple, etiologically-determined factors which are constitutional, genetic, psychogenetic, environmental, social, and cultural.

Many clinicians now use psychotropic agents with group therapies. Depressions are usually treated with anti-depressants and supportive psychotherapy. Endogenous depressions are clearly more effectively treated with anti-depressants. Reactive, situational and chronic characterological depressions are still difficult to treat. Psychotherapy is the treatment of choice in some. Some studies have shown that "no treatment" also works in 46 percent, though it is difficult to define no treatment or no help in a sickness. Psychotherapy is merely facilitated by anti-depressants in some patients.

Our educational enterprise has been polarized to various degrees relative to psychodynamics and psychopharmacology. Since we have no integrative comprehensive theory for the two ideological approaches, we must arrange, before it is too late, adequate systematic research comparing the efficacies of various treatments, separately and in combination. This can only be accomplished by trained researchers and clinicians in settings where rigid and critical standards can be maintained with adequate diagnostic and behavioral rating scale evaluations. Of course, informed consent by patient and family, with controls and changes over time, is necessary in appropriate psychiatric patients. We also need controlled clinical trials for the evaluation of drug-psychotherapy interactions. The projects in the literature have been quoted and questioned critically and some investigators are not happy with them. The errors in design need to be corrected. There are several research projects now funded in which the research design in combined pharmaco- and psychotherapy is just beginning. No systematic evidence exists that appropriate psychotropic agents at appropriate dosages interfere with the psychotherapy of schizophrenia. Much opinion exists in the literature, however. The current in-press Group for the Advancement of Psychiatry Report is the best reference to the matter under discussion.

The introduction of psychoactive drugs as an important addition to the treatment of depression and other affective disorders has altered the prognosis for depression and drastically changed the organization and treatment of programs with persons with affective disorders. Every psychiatrist and numerous other physician specialists will find it necessary to know the neuropsychology of the various classes of psychoactive drugs, i.e., minor and major tranquilizers, tricylic anti-depressants, monoamine oxidase inhibiting anti-depressants, knowledge of the mode of action and locus of action. The need for accurate knowledge of the side effects is exceeded only by the necessity for knowing specific indications as well as contraindications.

8

The Psychotherapy of Marital Partners: Old or New?

Peter A. Martin, M.D.

I. INTRODUCTION

The question asked in the title of this paper emphasizes two points. First, the field of marital therapy is chronologically both very old and very new. There has always been concern about the intimate relationship of husbands and wives. Yet the first clinics in the United States to begin serving couples with problems opened in the 1930's. The literature on marital therapies was meager before the 1950's, and only increased rapidly after 1960 (Olsen, 1970).

The second point emphasized by the title is quite different. It stems from the fact that there is neither a uniform theory nor a uniform clinical approach in the field of marital therapy. One would have to know the theoretical basis and the clinical approach of the therapist involved to know whether the psychotherapy being done was old or new. For example, much of the early literature referred to the work done with couples as *marriage counseling*. The manner in which the therapist distinguished counseling from psychotherapy determined the type of psychotherapy being used. Olsen (1970) noted correctly

125

that the global term marriage counseling does not adequately convey the range and variety of approaches to therapy with the marital dyad as it once did. In its place he proposed that the specific type of marital therapy be indicated.

We can apply this by utilizing the College's meeting format which is divided into four categories. If we use the same four categories for psychotherapy of marital problems, the therapy could be conducted along lines of: 1) Dyadic Psychotherapy, 2) Behavior Therapy, 3) Psychopharmacology in a Psychotherapeutic Setting, or 4) Group Therapy. I would add a fifth category—Comprehensive Psychotherapy. This would be a form of psychotherapy that takes into account not only individual intrapsychic and interpersonal vectors, but also the dimensions of family, extra-family group, and community relations. Thus, depending upon which of the above approaches was being used, any particular instance of marital therapy could either be old or new.

In a previous publication I have reviewed the literature and offered a critique (Martin 1970) of the various forms of psychotherapy of marital disharmony. Through 25 years of clinical experience with marital problems, I have experimented with most of the various types, specifically: 1) dynamic psychotherapy of one of the mates (Oberndorf 1938), 2) consecutive dynamic psychotherapy of marital partners (Oberndorf 1938), 3) concurrent psychotherapy of marital partners (Mittelmann 1948), 4) collaborative psychotherapy of marital partners (Martin and Bird 1953, Martin 1965), 5) conjoint psychotherapy (Jackson and Weakland 1961, Satir 1965, Watson 1962), 6) group therapy of marriage partners (Blender and Kirschenbaum 1967). As skill, experience, and experimentation increased, the therapies were conducted as indicated along the lines of the six categories mentioned above.

In this presentation I will draw conclusions and generalizations on 1) normal values for marriage and 2) harmonious marriages based on less than these "normal" values. Use of this "normal" value system allows for a diagnostic evaluation in marital therapy which unfortunately has received little attention in the literature. Proceeding from the diagnostic interviews which use these values as a theoretical base, psychotherapy of marriage problems moves towards modifying the psychopathological values uncovered in a particular marriage and towards a harmonious, working marriage.

II. Derivation of "Normal" Values for Marriage from Three Pathological Marriage Patterns

It is medical tradition to determine normal values of body functions as a derivative from prior investigation of abnormal functioning. Normal values for heart functioning followed years of treating diseases of the heart. Normal blood sugar values were recognized after working with diseases involving hyper- and hypoglycemia. When an organ of the body is functioning smoothly, there is often little incentive to study its mechanisms. When it gets out of order, our attention is called to those mechanisms responsible for its failure to function.

During the past 25 years, in working with patients who were extremely unhappy in their marriages, my attention was called to those mechanisms responsible for the failure of the marriage to function. Freud pointed out that the study of psychopathology has been of enormous service in contributing to our knowledge of the "normal" psychology of everyday life. Psychoanalysis has already made considerable progress in formulating scientific generalizations by making use of highlights which psychopathology can throw upon the dynamic mechanisms of normal behavior. Following are three marriage patterns which illustrate various mechanisms of psychopathology. From these I have derived "normal" values in healthy, smoothly running marriages.

A.   The "Love Sick" Wife and the "Cold Sick" Husband Marriage Pattern

This pattern is the most common and most difficult psychotherapeutic problem which we have encountered (Martin and Bird 1959). It would seem that this type of marriage problem is not confined to the American culture; requests for reprints came from all over the world.

The patients involved were those seen in the private practice of psychiatry with patients from the upper middle class socio-economic levels.

The husband's ability to afford simultaneous psychotherapy for himself and his wife represents an expression of the man's adequate talents and sufficient ego strength. It is this illustration of the strength of the ego which characterizes the husbands and is in marked contrast to the weakness of the wives' egos.

The Wives

The clinical entity is determined by the picture presented by the wives. No one wife illustrated all of the features to be enumerated, but when the individual variations of the theme were removed, the picture proved to be basically the same. The wife comes for treatment first because she has been experiencing severe anxiety, depressions, and incapacitating physical symptoms. She is no longer able to manage the home, care for the children, or discharge her social obligations. She may have been taking tranquilizers for years under the guidance of her family physician. She is emotionally decompensated and bordering on an even more severe regression. From the first interview with the psychiatrist, or as soon as the depression lifts in a depressed patient, she claims that her sickness is due entirely to the coldness and cruelty of her husband. She insists that he doesn't care about what she wants or what she feels. She states emphatically that she has a deep capacity to love, but that her husband is cold, unsympathetic, cruel, and psychotic, or even that he unconsciously wishes to kill her.

She gives countless examples to prove how emotionally inadequate he is by showing how he didn't do what he should have done, as evidence of his inability to love. She denies her intrapsychic conflicts by stressing the interpersonal relations. She either complains that her husband is sexually inadequate or oversexed. Her frigidity is either denied or blamed upon her husband. A stalemate in her treatment leads to the wife's statement that her husband must go into treatment too or she will not get well or a divorce will be necessary. To her, the only solution is a change in her husband. Her opinion, forcibly expressed, is that the husband, even though symptom free, is sicker than the wife. Sometimes, it is the inexperienced psychiatrist himself who makes this statement or the desperate psychiatrist who can't reach the wife and who must accept her conditions, hoping to effect some change in her through the husband.

These wives can be placed in the broad diagnostic category of borderline patients whose relation to their husbands is of a symbiotic, parasitic type. They suffer from the specific narcissistic problem of their self-esteem. They do not experience a fixed, firm, stable personality of their own as distinct from the need-satisfying objects. When in the presence of their husbands, these women look to them for approval to establish who they themselves are and how worthwhile they are.

The picture of these women is so characteristic that they are easy to recognize within a few minutes after the first hour has started and one can predict just what they are going to say for the rest of the hour. They can be recognized at any age group, even before marriage. I remember a 70-year-old woman who came because of a depression. She had been married 50 years, had children, grandchildren, and great grandchildren. I asked her what was troubling her. Her tale of woe was the same. Her husband didn't love her. He paid attention to other women, kidding and joking with waitresses when they went to restaurants.

High school girls have come, tearful and depressed because boyfriends do not pay enough attention to them. Little girls are reared differently from little boys. One of the ways is how they are received when they reach out for approval from adults. Girls who have a strong need for approval usually find it. It is acceptable behavior. But boys who need approval are scorned badly. Such experiences for girls ill prepare them for the pubertal, adolescent, and adult one-to-one relations with a man where her belief is that it is the responsibility of her husband to relieve all her anxieties, desires, and unfulfilled needs. Such an attitude serves only to arouse whatever dormant passive-resistant traits the men may have. They may treat the wives as they themselves were treated as children when they demanded love—with scorn.

To the male therapist, these wives as patients are tender traps. They are often vocal, emotional, enthusiastic, artistic, talented, attractive. They seem to make quick, strong, positive transferences to the therapist; they seem to believe so greatly in the value of treatment that they declare everyone should be in treatment, especially their husbands. They are hysterical personalities whose structures may be considered to be on a genital level, but who really are deeply-rooted oral characters.

The Husbands

The clinical picture of the husbands which completes this marital pattern varied markedly. The husbands were intelligent, educated men who held positions of responsibility. They were at least competent and some were even brilliant in their respective fields. They were respected in their work and in their communities. They were not emotionally decompensated and not given to drugs or alcohol. They differed from their wives radically in not showing much emotion. They were more intellectual, logical, and reasoning in their relationships to other people and problems. They were adequate to the requirements of life outside of the home, but varied in their adequacy within the home due to the wives' unrelenting involvements with them.

The greatest variation among the husbands lay in their own evaluation of a need for psychotherapy. At one extreme there were those who were adamant in the view that they needed no help and that the problem was entirely the wife's. Some of these wouldn't even come for an evaluation. The middle group was willing to do anything to alleviate the disturbed marital conditions and was eager for help for themselves. At the other extreme were some who were beginning to doubt their own senses and to think that perhaps their wives were right about the problems being entirely the fault of the husband.

During treatment, the picture presented by these men differed markedly from their wives' presentations. It was the picture of apparently well-adjusted men who had been successful in their occupational activities, in their social relationships, and in various ways when under pressure, which suggested that they were being emotionally mature to the degree of justifying inclusion in the broad classification of the so-called "normal" adult. Despite this classification, their treatment revealed that beneath the surface of their characteristic attitudes and defenses was a ferocity of emotional conflicts. There were great restrictions and even impoverishment of instinctual expressions and in some a prominence of primitive ego defenses. In some, the ferocity of the conflicts was as great as those of their wives. Why then were the wives sick and these men considered relatively healthy? The vital difference lies in their egos. While it may be true from the treatment of these men that normality may be considered to be a fiction or a fantasy, a person can be considered ego strong who, while defending himself against the drives, has not deprived himself of energy for the sustaining of ego functions in consonance with instinctual needs. If these men were judged by such a yardstick, then they varied markedly as to the degree of their ego strength. Some suffered by great restriction and impoverishment of their instinctual expression—especially in the expression of love. Their superegos and reality egos triumphed at the expense of a restriction of libido. They could be diagnosed as character neuroses. They had fixed, rigid character structures with a sense of personal continuity and systematization that was in marked contrast to their wives.

These are patients whom psychiatrists, in contrast to their reactions to the wives, frequently do not like. They either refuse to come for treatment or, in treatment, show little need or respect for the psychiatrist's help. They are often standoffish, suspicious, and, compared to the wives' rapid involvements, have a paranoid approach which may antagonize the inexperienced therapist.

The Marriage Pattern

These are marriages in which a reversal takes place after the marriage ceremony. At the onset of the marriage, the wife seems to have the upper hand. She is pretty or vivacious and the husband is plain, shy, or subdued. She appears to be exciting and entertaining or promises a knowledge of the arts, music, and the humanities which the husband lacks. During the years that follow, the husband continues to grow in character, becomes successful in business or profession, becomes more adequate in dealing with people, loses his shyness, and gains confidence in himself. He is a worker. The wife, in contrast, is a talker. Despite her protests, she does not feel motherly, does not enjoy responsibilities in the home, and is incapable of establishing herself outside of the home as she flits from one situation to another.

One Washington, D.C. journalist wrote a column stating that Washington in the evening is the most depressing city he has seen. At cocktail parties you meet couples whose presence is determined by the success of the husbands who have become leaders in their fields. The depressing picture was that of their wives. Even if the marriages had started with the mates as equals, the wives had not grown through the years and the contrast was appalling to the writer. In working with such wives, one discovers that it is appalling to them too. Their narcissistic supplies are depleted and they suffer devastating blows to their self-esteem, leading to varying defenses of depression, or overwhelming amounts of destructive energy that threatens dissolution of their egos or projection on to the husbands of the unacceptable portions of their own personalities.

The study of the wives' personalities and our conclusions early in our studies, as well as follow-up studies after 25 years, show an amazing consistency—a sameness with minor changes except for the few whose analyses were successful. In contrast, the pictures of some of the husbands after 25 years changed remarkably. As mentioned above, some continued to grow and develop in their careers through the years. Only in one small group (20 percent), who recognized no need for help, the methods which had brought them success early in life proved to be too rigid and inflexible. When there was need for change at work, they kept their same approach. They had been promoted above the level of their capacities. This, together with their relative inability to understand people's feelings, caused them difficulties at the higher level of their functioning. The early paranoid attitudes became intensified. With later life failures which men encounter in business, they became emotionally decompensated. Interestingly enough, in their group the accusations hurled at them by their wives early in the marriage and not clearly discernible by psychiatric evaluation gradually became clear. Within her paranoid projections were the kernels of truth. An individual may function well in many areas with no marked recognition of a problem with intimacy that is exposed early in the intensity of the marriage relationship.

B.   An "In-Search-of-a-Mother" Marital Pattern

In this specific entity, Martin and Bird (1962), the husband comes to the psychiatrist because a crisis has arisen in his marriage. He is having an affair with "another woman" and plans to marry her. External circumstances have blocked his plans and precipitate his breakdown. When he comes to the psychiatrist on his own, it is mainly to find out how to get that which he wants so desperately. Some of these men do not come willingly, but are forced to do so by their angry wives who now refuse to take them back without psychotherapy.

The picture of the men involved with this type of problem breaks down into two groups. The active or mastering group is made up of individuals with a tendency to be successful in whatever they do. They cannot conceive of defeat in their wishes to marry their paramours. They wish to borrow the fantasied "know-how" from the psychiatrist. They cannot stand feelings of helplessness and break down or become depressed only when it becomes evident they will not get what they want.

The passive, dependent group search for mothering as a manifestation of their regressive, demanding positions. They are in search of loving and protection. They do not manage their affairs well, compete poorly with other men, and turn to women for consolation. They border on irresponsibility and impulsiveness. Alcoholism is a common symptom in this group.

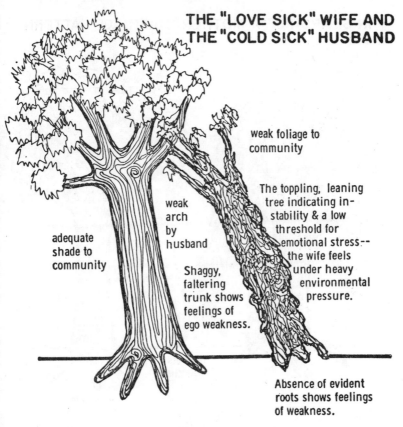

THE "LOVE SICK" WIFE AND THE "COLD SICK" HUSBAND

weak foliage to community

weak arch by husband

adequate shade to community

Shaggy, faltering trunk shows feelings of ego weakness.

The toppling, leaning tree indicating instability & a low threshold for emotional stress-- the wife feels under heavy environmental pressure.

Absence of evident roots shows feelings of weakness.

Figure 1

Characteristics of the Wives

These wives are characteristically excellent mothers. They all state that they love their husbands and do show a capacity to endure traumatic marital experiences. Divorces are rare as they usually accept the return of the husbands. They note that change in the marriage occurred when the children came and they were no longer able to devote themselves exclusively to the husbands.

"IN SEARCH OF A MOTHER" MARRIAGE PATTERN

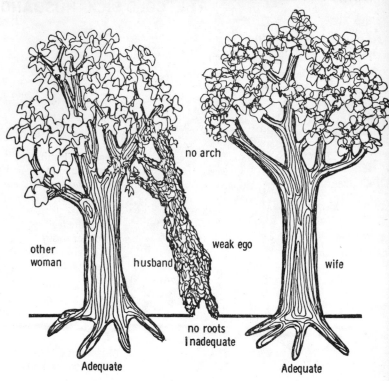

Figure 2

Characteristics of the "Other Women"

They are capable, competent individuals and, if married, are capable mothers and wives in their own right. Their involvement with these men seems based on their response to a needy person. Also, the marriage often would mean social and economic improvement. In addition, these men tend to be excellent lovers, with great capacity for physical intimacy. Nevertheless, when final decisions are to be made, these women are more realistic than the men, and, if married, often refuse to divorce their husbands. Their children are more important than their lovers. If unmarried or widowed, they are willing to marry the husband. Here we have a different picture. Now the wife comes for treatment to find out how to recapture her husband from the "other woman."

The Marriage Pattern

The pattern is not uncommon. The man marries young, even before he is done with his training or able to earn a living. He appears to marry for love. His wife works and helps him in his career until the children come. Simultaneous with her inability to take complete care of him, he becomes financially self-sufficient and looks for another woman who will be free to take good care of him—one who may be younger, prettier and more sensuous.

C. THE "DOUBLE-PARASITE" MARITAL PATTERN

These were marriages of two people who cannot swim, clutching each other desperately and drowning together.

The couples seen who fit this pattern came from two extremes. Some were seen in a "free-clinic" out-patient psychiatry department of a general hospital. They were indigents. Neither partner was able to carry the load of the marriage. Alcoholism, drugs, anxiety, depression, and inability to work characterized these couples. The other couples of this group were seen in private practice and were very wealthy. However, the wealth had been inherited either by one or both mates. They were emotionally incapable of handling the responsibilities of their education and position, incapable of being good parents, and hostilely projecting their inadequacies onto the mate. They were filled with anxieties and neurotic symptoms as defenses. The two living together didn't quite make one ego. They made a parasitic

THE DOUBLE PARASITE PATTERN

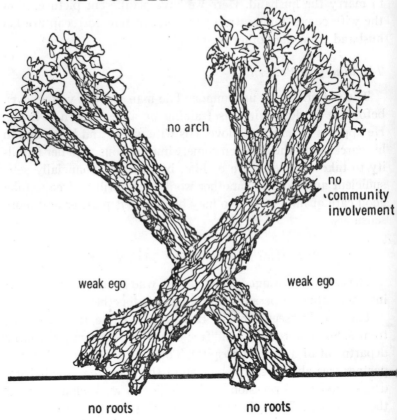

Figure 3

duo of two cactuses who could not live together and also could not live alone.

Having described three psychopathological marriage patterns, I am now ready to derive values for a "normal" marriage.

D. The "Normal" Marriage

To illustrate the "normal" marriage, visualize in your mind's eye driving down a city street on a hot summer's day with the sun beating down on you. Suddenly you look to the side and see a street with a row of trees on each side whose branches and leaves form an *arch* which makes a sheltered, cool, peaceful shady lane. The trees also give shade to the sidewalks and houses—children can be seen playing in this peaceful setting. The trees on each side are deeply rooted in the soil, sturdy and upright in their growth, and in forming the arch together create something which neither tree could do alone. Underneath the earth their roots may be intertwined.

In the studies which accompanied Action For Mental Health several years ago, one section dealt with the definition of mental health. It proved difficult to define. But the minimal definition of mental health in the American culture was the ability to stand on your own two feet without too much imposition upon others. In addition a marriage creates an arch which neither individual can do alone. A healthy marriage then is a union between two self-supporting and supportive-of-others individuals who are committed to their marriage union. These "normal" values for marriage are based on psychoanalytic concepts of psychosocial development from the early symbiotic mother-child relationship through separation and individuation to maturity, wisdom, knowledge and the capacity to feel kinship with and love for human beings other than oneself. Ideally in marriage independence is equal, dependence mutual and obligations reciprocal but there are many variations from this ideal (as will

THE HEALTHY MARRIAGE

Strong trunk-- shows self-con- fidence & strong ego.

Strong arch formed by both trees. Trees stand upright showing stability & ability to stand environmental pressures.

Deep roots denote strong sense of identity & feelings of strength.

Figure 4

be shown later) which still allow for a working marriage. Normal values here, as in other areas of human functions, allow for wide ranges before becoming pathological. Marriage, of course, is not a static state but is one phase of the individual's life cycle. It is one wherein further growth and development can occur through the intimate experience with the mate. It is a state in which marriage partners can help one another to reach the full status of being responsible and autonomous human beings; however, the intensity of the relationship can also cause regression and psychopathology. It has the capacity for growth or destructiveness.

The preceding four sketches are graphic presentations of the three pathologic marriages and the healthy marriage pattern derived from them.

The four sketches recapitulate the previous material. Points to be reemphasized are as follows.

In the above sketch of the "normal" marriage (Figure 4), each tree stands upright showing stability and ability to stand up to environmental pressures. The strong trunks show self-confidence and a strong ego. The deep roots denote a strong sense of identity and feelings of strength. A strong, functional arch is formed by the boughs of both trees. When the arch holds, all else holds together. Love in marriage cements the arch —hate breaks the arch. "Hate and pride break arches. Love and understanding build unbreakable arches." (Sandberg, 1957).

In Figure 1 we see the husband giving adequate shade to the community but leaning away from his wife and contributing sparsely to the arch. His roots are deeply embedded in the soil. In contrast, in the "love sick" wife symbolization there is an absence of roots, showing feelings of weakness, and the toppling, leaning trunk indicates instability and a low threshhold for emotional stress. The shaggy, faltering trunk shows feelings of ego weakness. Her involvement with making a marriage arch is in contrast to her weak foliage toward community involvement and love of mankind.

Figure 2 shows both the wife and the "other" woman as adequate, self-sufficient individuals, with the weak-egoed, weak-rooted husband leaning away from the wife and not contributing to the formation of an arch. He has no community involvement.

Figure 3 shows the two weak-egoed, rootless, and shadeless

trees leaning against each other and contributing nothing to the community. This type of pseudomutuality forms no arch.

The "normal" marriage, then, involves a relationship between two equally self-supporting and supportive adults. Obviously this ideal is never present 100 percent in nature. It is a reference point which helps to explain both adequate functioning and malfunctioning. No person remains the same in each stage of his life cycle. And although all men are created equal, some are more equal than others. There are some trees which are taller and give more shade than others, but the others are still sufficient unto themselves. In general, a mutual commitment to each other forms an arch in marriage that allows for a protected, comfortable street on hot, stormy, snowy, windy, violent days. The arch creates a haven from the elements, where the children know that they are cherished.

III.   Normal Values Derived from Psychopathology in the Sexual Aspects of Marriage

The preceding material developed "normal" values for marriage with little mention of sexual problems. In the present era of the sexual revolution, treatment of marriage problems rarely occurs without concomitant treatment of sexual problems. Experience has indicated that sexual problems can best be understood and then treated by the recognition of three dominant areas and their varying influences and combinations.

A) Intercourse per se, without physical or emotional intimacy (lust). This aspect involves a physical discharge of libidinal drive.

B) Physical intimacy (sensuousness). This involves sensuous pleasures (touching, kissing, petting, etc.) pre and post intercourse. There has been a tremendous increase in emphasis on sensuousness in the mass media and by experts in sexuality. Sensitivity training groups flourish throughout America, stressing aspects of intimacy and particularly freedom to experience pleasures in physical intimacies without intercourse.

C) *Emotional intimacy* (*love*). Love of course is a difficult condition to define let alone explain. Salzman (1973) distinguishes it from infatuation, which he defines as very self-oriented, a wild ecstatic feeling of having fallen in love, or a fantasy about being in love. Individuals are initially drawn to people by outward characteristics and only later discover deeper qualities which are desired, or later do not discover deeper qualities and hate may develop instead of love. Salzman defines mature love as a state of being where the satisfaction or security of another person becomes as important as one's own. This is a sure expression of intimacy, tenderness and a collaborative relationship with another human being. Thus, it may be considered that true love develops prior to the maturation of the sexual function and is uncomplicated by lust. Love recognizes the strivings of the other person and preserves the other's integrity as an individual self.

With this prelude, I will present clinical material involving pathology in the areas of intercourse, sensuousness, and emotional intimacy. From the clinical material, I will derive a set of normal values in marriage for these three aspects of sexuality.

I will not touch here upon the important area of taking a sexual history. The previous absence of literature in this area has been alleviated by a recent publication of GAP (Group For The Advancement of Psychiatry 1973).

Variations on Three Sexual Themes Encountered in Treatment of Marriage Problems

A. Sex—intercourse per se (lust), without physical (sensuousness) or emotional intimacy (love)

1) *Wife*: "My husband is like a truck driver. He comes home, we have intercourse. No talking, no lovemaking. No prepara-

tion, no love. He is an animal. All he wants is intercourse. I can't stand it."

2) *Husband*: "My wife says that she cannot stand me anymore. She wants no intimacy. When I demand it, she will have intercourse. No preliminary, no foreplay, no talking. She lets me have intercourse with her and that is it. No response on her part. But she does her duty. I can't stand it."

B. Intimacy—emotional (love) and physical (sensuousness) without intercourse or response during intercourse

1) *Wife*: "He is a great lover. Foreplay goes on for hours. He uses his hands, mouth, and every part of my body. But he doesn't have intercourse with me. He must be afraid of it. I don't know what I will do if he doesn't have intercourse with me."

2) *Husband*: "She is great on kissing and holding and hugging and talking romantically. But she can't respond in intercourse. She can't have an orgasm. I can stimulate her by the hour and she never can let go. I have lost confidence in myself. I would love to have the experience of a woman responding to me. I wonder if I could still do that. I would rather be with a prostitute than with her. She doesn't really love me."

C. No sex (lust); no intimacy, physical (sensuousness) or emotional (love)

1) *Wife*: "On our honeymoon he brought ten books. He doesn't talk to me, he doesn't make love to me, he doesn't have intercourse with me. I have to beg him for intercourse. I think there must be something wrong with me. I am so furious, I think I am going crazy. If I'm not careful in what I say, his feelings get hurt all the time. I wish I had married a truck driver."

2) *Husband*: "She treats me like dirt. Touching her is like

touching an icicle. No talking, no kissing, no sex. I have turned
to masturbation and have fantasies of other women. I know I
am going to have an affair."

From the above pathology we can derive a picture of sexual
normality: an individual who can combine the pleasures of emotional and physical intimacy with the pleasure of adequate intercourse. This is an adult who has triumphed against the odds
and emerged a winner. Apparently it is a rare breed. It does not
happen as often as we wish it would, but it is at least an ideal,
a goal to be achieved. In psychotherapy, once the diagnosis is
made by these guidelines, efforts are made to bring about
changes in the desired direction.

IV. VARIATIONS FROM "NORMAL" VALUES IN FUNCTIONING
MARRIAGES AND CONCLUSIONS THEREFROM

An ideal marriage from the sexual standpoint would be a
matching up of two such individuals. But what of those who
have not achieved the ideal? Such match-ups still occur in nature, whether by choice or by chance. These are not the ones
who complain. They are not the ones who come for treatment.
Less than ideal, but workable couplings would be as follows:

A. *Lust Minus Sensuousness and Love*

A highly (intercourse-minded) sexual male, lacking in capacity for emotional or physical intimacy, married to a woman
with the same combination. The sexual union appears to be the
bond which keeps them together. They may fight and scream all
day long, but it doesn't interfere with their bedtime union which
keeps the marriage palatable.

B. *Sensuousness and Love Minus Lust*

A husband and wife who are affectionate, loving, considerate
of one another all day long, but not strongly motivated for in-

tercourse. His quickness to ejaculate doesn't bother her since it keeps him happy and he doesn't expect a response from her which she feels incapable of experiencing. Vital needs are few; expectations are low.

C. Low Sensuousness, Lust and Love

A low intimacy and low sex life marital pair whose low key approach allows for what may appear to be a cold marriage, but one which is workable for them. Needs and expectations are minimal.

What valid conclusions can be made from this material drawn from less than ideal but functioning marriages? In effect, these marriages are functioning with fewer functional areas than some of the pathological marriage illustrations of the preceding few paragraphs. The generalization can be made (which is validated by clinical experience) that marital disharmony is a manifestation of dis-ease in the marital relationship between two human beings. The dis-ease is a result of expectations in one or both partners which are not gratified by the other. Where expectations are mutually gratified, health results. Where there are few expectations and few disappointments, functional marriages with an absence of dis-ease result.

Thus the problem is one of proper matching up of couples prior to marriage, or of adjustments during the marriage. The basis of this is the marriage contract.

V. The Marriage Contract

Experience shows that the marriage contract involves a conscious and unconscious set of terms. When the conscious and unconscious expectations mesh, marital harmony is assured. When the conscious contract is understood and agreed upon by both but there is an unconscious disagreement in one or both partners, dis-ease results. Psychotherapy is directed to exposing the contracts and changing those parts that are dissonant, either between the conscious and unconscious of an individual or between the conscious and/or unconscious of the couple.

Some individuals are dishonest in the making of the conscious contract! They agree (in order to get married) to things they have no intention of doing; immediately after the ceremony, they start changing the terms, often with disastrous results.

It has been the contention of some psychiatrists that divorces do not help because the individual again marries a person with the same problems. Normative studies do not bear this out. They show that many people do learn and in second marriages make different match-ups or change their expectations, resulting in workable marriages.

VI. SUMMARY

The following chart is a summarization of the preceding material.

THE "NORMAL" VALUE SYSTEM OF DIAGNOSIS OF MARITAL DISHARMONY

Capacities measured during initial interviews leading to formulation of tentative diagnosis and plan of psychotherapy.

A. *Individually—(each partner)*

   1. Capacity for independence (to stand alone)
   2. Capacity for supportiveness (to mate)
   3. Capacity to accept support (from mate)
   4. Capacity for lust (intercourse)
   5. Capacity for sensuousness (physical intimacy)
   6. Capacity for love (emotional intimacy)

B.   The Marriage Contract

    1. Conscious contract
        a. Areas of agreement
        b. Areas of disagreement

    2. Unconscious contract
        a. Areas of agreement
        b. Areas of disagreement

Psychotherapy of marital disharmony follows from diagnosis of areas of incompatibility, with an attempt to rectify them by one or more of the many techniques available.

VII.   CONCLUSIONS

This paper gives recognition to the reality that the type of psychotherapy used in any particular instance is determined by the therapist involved. However, the type of therapy is not considered the most important issue. Primary is a diagnosis of the problems prior to therapy. This paper contributes to the literature a theoretical basis for a comprehensive approach to psychotherapy of marital partners by establishing "normal" psychological values for marriage derived from experience with psychopathologic marriages. These "normal values" chosen for guidelines involve independence, supportiveness, acceptance of support, lust, sensuousness and love as important strands in the cord of the relationship between marriage partners.

Using their "normal" values as guidelines during the initial diagnostic interviews, psychotherapy proceeds from diagnosis to effecting a normalization of the pathological values. This aims toward a homeostatic balance. There are many psychotherapic techniques useful to achieve this goal. As Masters and Johnson have shown, sometimes rectifying sexual areas balances the marriage. There is no magic in any one technique. Technique is often something one tries when an understanding of the problems present has not been achieved. The understanding is the prime requisite from which therapy flows naturally. Recognition is also given to the importance of concordance between the conscious and unconscious contracts between mates. If therapy cannot effect terms to which both parties can commit themselves, failure will occur because of an impossible match-up of mates. The same individual who fails with one mate can be a match-up with a different mate.

Hollender (1971) elucidated clearly the nature of marital problems in emphasizing that the comfort or discomfort, the durability or disruption, and the success or failure of a marriage have little to do with the normality or neurosis of either partner. As was illustrated by clinical material in this paper, it is the dovetail of needs that is decisive. Reciprocal needs foster a good fit, clashing ones result in disharmony. Hollender also adds these factors to be considered in viewing marital relationships: 1) attitude towards problems, 2) expectations of partners, 3) manner in which the marital relationship is used or exploited, 4) the attitude towards marital and family stability.

Therapy is then directed to reestablishing a former fit, creating a new fit, creating a fit for the first time, or recognizing that no fit is possible with a particular couple. A mutually satisfying, interlocking, homeostatic balance is sought that gratifies both mature and neurotic needs of both partners. The therapist, by whatever techniques he uses, aids in this mutual search. This is the desired therapeutic alliance in marital therapy.

REFERENCES

BLENDER, M. G. and KIRSCHENBAUM, M. The Technique of Married Couple Group Therapy. *Archives of General Psychiatry*, 17:44-52. 1967.

GROUP FOR THE ADVANCEMENT OF PSYCHIATRY. Assessment of Sexual Function: A Guide to Interviewing. Vol. VIII, Report No. 88, 1973.

HOLLENDER, M. H. Selection of Therapy for Marital Problems. In *Current Psychiatric Therapies*, Vol. II, J. H. Masserman, ed., pp. 119-127. New York: Grune and Stratton, 1971.

JACKSON, D. D. and WEAKLAND, J. H. Conjoint Family Treatment. *Psychiatry*, 24:30-45, 1961.

MARTIN, P. A. Treatment of Marital Disharmony by Collaborative Therapy. In *The Psychotherapies of Marital Disharmony*, B. L. Green, ed., pp. 83-191. New York: The Free Press, 1965.

MARTIN, P. A. An Historical Survey of the Psychotherapy of Marriage Partners. Chapter 6 in *Hope: Psychiatry's Commitment*. A. D. R. Sipe, ed. New York: Brunner/Mazel, 1970.

MARTIN, P. A. and BIRD, H. W. An Approach to the Psychotherapy of Marriage Partners: The Stereoscopic Technique. *Psychiatry*, 16: 123-127. 1953.

MARTIN, P. A. and BIRD, H. W. The "Love Sick" Wife and the "Cold Sick" Husband. *Psychiatry*, 22:246. 1959.

MARTIN, P. A. and BIRD, H. W. One Type of the "In-Search-of-a-Mother." Marital Pattern. *Psychiatric Quarterly*, 36:283-293, 1962.

MITTELMANN, B. The Concurrent Analysis of Married Couples. *Psychoanalytic Quarterly*, 17:182-197, 1948.

OBERNDORF, C. P. Psychoanalysis of Married Couples. *International Journal of Psychoanalysis*, 25:450, 1938.

OLSEN, D. H. Marital and Family Therapy: Integrative Review and Critique. *Journal of Marriage and the Family*, November, pp. 501-536, 1970.

SANDBERG, C. Remembrance Rock. In *The Sandberg Range*. New York: Harcourt, Brace & Co., 1957, p. 233.

SALZMAN, L. Discussion. *Medical Aspects of Human Sexuality*. February, 1973, p. 108.

SATIR, V. M. Conjoint Marital Therapy. In *Psychotherapy of Marital Disharmony*, Bernard L. Greene, ed. New York: The Free Press, 1965.

WATSON, A. S. The Conjoint Psychotherapy of Marriage Partners. *Am. J. Psychiatry*, pp. 912-922, 1962.

Part III

THE STANLEY R. DEAN AWARD LECTURE

9

A Biometric Approach to Diagnosis and Evaluation of Therapeutic Intervention in Schizophrenia

Joseph Zubin, Ph.D.

In honoring me with the Stanley R. Dean Award, the American College of Psychiatrists and Fund for the Behavioral Sciences are recognizing not only my own contribution to the study of schizophrenia, but that of our entire Biometrics Research Unit established in January 1956, exactly 17 years ago, by the late Dr. Paul H. Hoch, then Commissioner of Mental Hygiene of the State of New York. The mandate received for this Unit was to develop an objective assessment of the behavior of the mentally ill with the purpose of improving diagnosis, prognosis, and evaluation of treatment and outcome*. Some of the contributions of this unit will be the substance of this chapter.

---

* The unit viewed its mandate through a wide-angled lens which included problems requiring the efforts of the following nine sections, each with its own staff and head, which were gradually added to the unit: (1) Anthropology, Dr. Muriel Hammer; (2) Behavior Analysis and Modification, Dr. Kurt Salzinger; (3) Biostatistics, Dr. Joseph L. Fleiss; (4) Diagnosis and Psychopathology, Dr. Barry J. Gurland; (5) Evaluation, Dr. Robert L. Spitzer; (6) Family Research, Dr. Denise Kandel; (7) Gerontology, Dr. Ruth Bennett; (8) Psychophysiology, Dr. Samuel Sutton, and (9) Sociology, Dr. David Wilder.

Many readers probably wonder what biometrics has to do with psychiatry and how such strange bedfellows as measurement and clinical research ever got together. Yet we have had a biometric tradition in psychiatry at least since the days of Esquirol, one of the first to count the number of patients according to the precipitating cause of their illness, finding some 25% were "love casualties." Jaspers (1) noted the importance of biometrics, as did Kraepelin (2) and Freud.

Freud's interest in the biometric approach is exemplified in his correspondence with Fliess (May 25, 1895). He writes: "I am plagued with two ambitions: to see how the theory of mental functioning takes shape if *quantitative* considerations, a sort of economics of nerve-force, are introduced into it . . ." This ambition culminated in his Project for a Scientific Psychology (3). Originally he believed that measurable physical-chemical forces in the neurons underlay human behavior and they were sufficient to explain behavior without recourse to extraneous unquantifiable forces. While he gave up some of this belief later because of his inability to explain hysteria on a physical-chemical basis alone, his early efforts had a strong biometric undertone. This trend in attempts at measuring the energy of the neuron also characterized the early work of the New York State Psychiatric Institute when it was established before the turn of the century. Van Gieson and Sidis in 1898 developed a rather complex neuronic energy model to explain normal and abnormal behavior (4).

In the '20s the first application of biometric methods to psychopathology was the testing of Henry Cotton's focal infection theory (5), which was demolished through the work of Kopeloff and Cheney (6) in the first clinical trial of a therapeutic method in psychiatry.

There followed a period of relative stagnation in biometric activity, until World War II opened the opportunities for biometric investigations through the support of federal funds. Now, a number of centers exist in which biometric activities are pursued, notably at NIMH in the Biometric Branch under the guidance of Dr. Morton Kramer.

There are certain prerequisites for the biometric approach to a given problem. We must have at least an operational definition of the area under investigation and reliable and valid objective tools for carrying out the investigation. It is not easy to further define the biometric approach to psychopathology. Essentially it derives from the dicta of Lord Kelvin, who postulated that unless you can measure something, you do not understand it, and from Thorndike, who postulated that whatever exists, exists in some amount, and therefore ought to be measurable.

In the early '30s I entered the field of psychopathology, fresh with a Ph.D. in psychology, and bringing the tools of experimental methods and design, statistical techniques, and mathematical reasoning with me to my first job at the Psychiatric Institute, ready to apply them to the mentally ill. But I soon faced the hard reality that the philosophy then current was psychoanalysis, which had no room for measurement, and even considered it a threat to treatment.

Despite this prevalent *zeitgeist*, I managed to take a few tentative steps into the field. When I was still a graduate student I dared, with the help of a few colleagues, to attempt a test of the tenability of one of Freud's fundamental assumptions—the Oedipus Situation. We tried to develop a test which would examine the relative preference of children for parents of the same or opposite sex. Among the test items were such as, "Suppose you were out in a canoe with both of them and could only save one, whom would you save?" The results indicated that Freud was right; namely, up to about age 6 there was a definite preference for the parent of the opposite sex and at age 6, apparently, the latency period had set in and even the girls preferred mother. We waited for a long time after sending all this material, together with statistical tables, to Freud before receiving his answer: *"ganz amerikanisch,* but I do not quite see what you can prove with your statistics." Taken aback by this refusal to accept verification, I inquired of some of my psychoanalytic friends as to what might have been the difficulty. I was told: "Suppose you came to the Pope with proof that God exists. What do you suppose he'd say?"

I then turned my attention to the most frequently used clinical tools of the '30s and '40s: self-report inventories, projective techniques, handwriting analysis, and sorting tests. I found each of these wanting, not because they were intrinsically invalid, but because of two basic difficulties: (a) responses to these techniques depended on the unique history of the individual and its reflection of the particular ecological niche in which he had developed, and (b) there was an absence of any criteria other than the clinical interview for validating the findings of these techniques. Even the value of the Rorschach technique vanished when it was regarded as a test (7).

The clinical interview, despite its primary usefulness in determining the presence or absence of psychopathology, was itself extremely unreliable, as many studies had shown. If it were to be used as the criterion for evaluating more objective aspects of behavior, it would have to become more objective and reliable. Thus, our Biometric Research Unit began to develop systematic structured interviews in which each question was accompanied by several possible response items. The presence or absence of each item could be recorded by the interviewer.

The mental status schedule, which had been the psychiatrist's mainstay, was converted into this kind of systematic structured interview in our laboratory, yielding high reliability in scoring of items, as well as considerable validity. We worked with three types of interviews: (a) a non-probing approach—Structured Clinical Interview (SCI) by Burdock and Hardesty (8); (b) a medium-probing—Mental Status Schedule (MSS) by Spitzer, Burdock, and Hardesty (9), and Psychiatric Status Schedule (PSS) by Spitzer, Endicott, Fleiss, and Cohen (10); and (c) a deep-probing—Present State Examination (PSE) by Wing, Birley, Cooper, Graham, and Isaacs (11).

Another reason we tried to objectify the clinical interview and render it more reliable and valid arose from our comparative international studies of diagnoses of mental disorder in the United States and the United Kingdom, undertaken by the Section on Diagnosis and Psychopathology of our unit. Faced with the report by Dr. Kramer (12) that the rate for manic-depressive psychosis was 10 times higher in the U.K. than in the U.S., and that the rate of schizophrenia, on the other hand, was much higher in the U.S. than in the U.K., we launched a study to determine the causes of this differential.

Using a combined schedule of non-probing, medium-probing, and deep-probing items, our Project on Diagnosis of Mental Disorders in the United Kingdom and the United States* was able to demonstrate that the much heralded differences in the incidence of hospitalized functional mental disorders (schizophrenia versus affective psychosis) in the United States and the United Kingdom were actually labeling differences (13, 14).

It appears that though British and American psychiatrists are equally sensitive to the presence of psychopathology in mental patients, American psychiatrists are inclined to use the label "schizophrenia" more and the label "affective disorders" less than the British.

One of the incidental, but most exciting, results of the development of systematic structured interviews and their application to large groups of mental patients is the possibility of laying down a new anatomy of psychopathology by dissecting out its underlying dimensions through statistical techniques such as factor analysis or typological analysis. Such an analysis yielding

---

* Headed by Dr. Barry Gurland in the United States and Dr. John Cooper, now succeeded by Dr. John Copeland, in the United Kingdom.

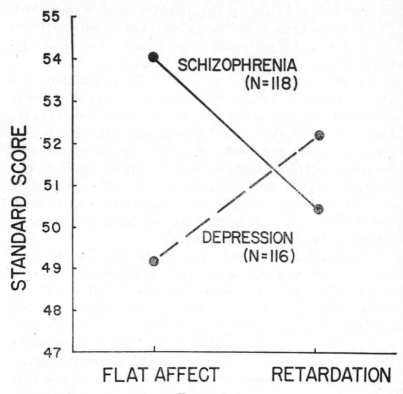

FIGURE 1
Underlying Dimensions of Flat Affect and Retardation for
Schizophrenia and Depression.

25 dimensions of psychopathology was achieved by Dr. Fleiss, head of the Section on Biostatistics of our unit (14a). As a result, we succeeded for the first time in separating anxiety from depression, two factors which ordinarily ran inseparably together in previous factor analyses.

Of special interest to schizophrenia are such factors as flat affect, retarded speech, and retarded movement. These three factors tended to merge into a single dimension in previous factor analyses. In our study, we succeeded in separating these factors in two. The key items in the flat affect factor are:

"Patient maintains a facial expression lacking signs of emotions,"
"Absence of normal variation in patient's tone of voice," and
"Patient talks of his condition with no outward sign of emotions."

The key items in the retardation factor are:
"Patient pauses a long time before replying to questions,"
"Patient walks abnormally slowly," and
"Patient speaks slowly."

To facilitate comparisons between diagnostic groups, all scores were standardized to a mean of 50 and a standard deviation of 10. These diagnoses were the final diagnoses arrived at by the project team of the U.S.-U.K. diagnostic study.

Figure 1 presents mean standard scores for all schizophrenics and all depressives. The difference between the two groups on retardation is small ($t=1.10$ [not significant]). The schizophrenics scored significantly higher than the depressives on flat affect, however ($t=3.35$, $p < .01$). It is thus the flat affect component of apathy and lethargy, and not the retardation component, which helps in distinguishing between schizophrenia and depression.

Figure 2 illustrates how the retardation component is important in separating depressives into neurotic and psychotic subtypes. The psychotic depressives score significantly higher than the neurotic depressives on retardation ($t = 3.07$, $p < .01$), but were not significantly different on flat affect ($t = 0.97$, [not significant]).

Both flat affect and psychomotor retardation are important for diagnostic discriminations. The means now exists to measure each without contamination by the other.

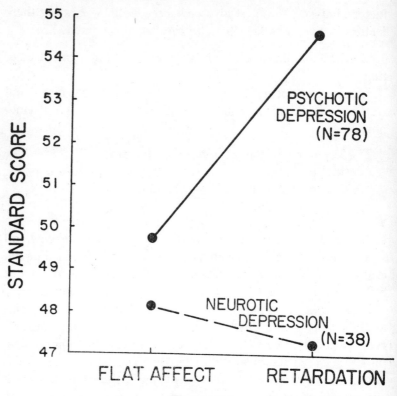

FIGURE 2
Underlying Dimensions of Flat Affect and Retardation
in Separating Psychotic and Neurotic Depressives.

The Evaluation Section of our unit under the direction of Drs. Spitzer and Endicott has developed standardized techniques for evaluating psychopathology and role functioning of patients and nonpatients to facilitate (a) comparing patient and nonpatient populations with regard to current and past mental health status, prognosis, and diagnosis; (b) evaluating different treatment programs and approaches; and (c) studying other substantive issues of etiology, treatment, and course of mental disorders.

These techniques have been shown to discriminate among subgroups of schizophrenics and to differentiate schizophrenics from other diagnostic groups. Two computer programs for diagnosis have been developed, each taking the results of psychiatric examinations as input. The program acts like a clinician in asking a series of questions of the data, and then yields a psychiatric diagnosis. The computer-derived psychiatric diagnoses have been shown to have a high agreement with clinical diagnoses made from the same data.

I have, thus far, indicated how our Biometrics Research Unit came to be interested in the better description of schizophrenia. Let us now go further in developing the topic of the evaluation of therapeutic intervention.

Therapeutic intervention may be defined as planned treatment of a disorder with the view to eliminating, or mitigating, or arresting its progress. To intervene effectively, we must first know (a) the nature and identity of the disorder, (b) the point in time at which to intervene, (c) how to intervene, (d) the method to use most effectively, and (e) how to evaluate the efficacy of intervention.

We must confess at the very start that when we look at the five areas of knowledge which we require, we are, in fact, facing voids. We do not know the nature of the disorder labeled schizophrenia; we cannot diagnose it accurately; we do not know the ideal moment to intervene or how to intervene, what method to use or how to evaluate it. Although we are abysmally ignorant, we must make do with whatever pragmatic knowledge practitioners have collected in the course of time. But we must not accept them at face value. It is necessary to lay bare the knowledge we have inherited in order to examine its tenability.

As far as the nature of the disorder is concerned and how it is to be identified, we must attempt to provide a definition if we are to communicate with others regarding the results of our investigations. As all of us are aware, no common agreement exists universally regarding mental disorders and especially regarding schizophrenia. How can this impasse be surmounted?

First, is it really necessary to provide an ironclad definition of schizophrenia? Is it necessary that a category be defined rigidly in a closed-ended way, like a mathematical concept? If this were necessary, such widely useful concepts as "species" would go by the board. Julian Huxley (15) has pointed out that: ". . . there is no single criterion of species. Morphological difference; failure to interbreed; infertility of offspring; ecological, geographical, or genetical distinctness—all those must be taken into account, but none of them singly is decisive. Failure to interbreed or to produce fertile offspring is the nearest approach to a positive criterion. It is, however, meaningless in apogamous forms, and as a negative criterion it is not applicable, many obviously distinct species, especially of plants, yielding fertile offspring, often with free Mendelian recombination on crossing. A combination of criteria is needed, together with some sort of *flair*."

If biologists cannot define species rigorously, we need not be shamefaced that we cannot rigorously define schizophrenia. The test of a good definition is not ironclad rigor, but usefulness.

Second, we must distinguish between the presence and absence of a disorder in general. We might regard a disorder as a progressive condition which, unless adequately dealt with, will result in premature death, severe loss of efficiency, or severe reduction of happiness (or increase in excessive pain), or some, or all of these. A disorder is to be distinguished from a defect, which is a stationary condition that will result in severe loss of efficiency or in a reduction of happiness or both, but will not necessarily shorten life.

It is simple enough to accept premature death as a criterion of a disorder, but it is not a very useful one since it can be used only retrospectively (though it may be possible in the future to utilize this criterion by means of suitable prognostic indicators). The criteria based on loss of efficiency and reduction of happiness are difficult to apply since these criteria have no readily available baseline.

One suggestion for circumventing these difficulties* is to utilize the value judgment that society places on the condition in question. Thus, if most possessors of a given condition would gladly be rid of it or are actively searching for ways of eliminating it, we could utilize this information as an index for the presence of a disorder. The inverse is particularly illuminating: a disorder is a condition which most of those not possessing it would neither seek nor be willing to accept.

Another index of the presence of a disorder** is whether society is sufficiently troubled by the condition to provide methods for eliminating it or containing it, or is actively searching for such methods.

Thus, a disorder is an undesirable state from which relief is sought. Whether this definition is to be locally applied in each subculture or whether a universal classification is to be developed remains an open question. If methods for eliminating or containing a condition are universally provided or sought, the recognition of this state as a disorder offers no problem. If only a small group of individuals or some highly isolated culture regards a given condition as a disorder, it would probably not be generally accepted as such. Between these extremes is a continuum of growing consensus as to whether a given condition is to be regarded as a disorder, and the higher the consensus across cultures, the greater the probability of its acceptance. Thus, the term disorder, like the term species, has no rigorous definition. "A combination of criteria is needed together with some sort of flair." (15)

---

* Suggested by Dr. Robert L. Spitzer of our unit.
**Suggested by Dr. Barry Gurland of our unit.

Concerning schizophrenia, it is clear that it satisfies four of our criteria for being regarded as a disorder: it interferes severely with efficient living; it severely reduces happiness; those who don't have it don't seek it, and those who do have it generally wish to be rid of it; and wherever it is recognized, some treatment for it is sought.

For operational purposes, glossaries have been developed which specify characteristic behaviors that must be present for a given condition of a patient to qualify as schizophrenia. There are several such glossaries available and it is hoped that we will eventually accept a universal glossary such as the one proposed by the World Health Organization (16) that will serve the purposes of better communication across different nations and cultures.

The aim of such a glossary should be to ensure so far as possible that those who use it will apply diagnostic terms uniformly. Thus, it is less important that the diagnostic terms be "correct" than that like conditions should be classified under the same rubric, and that it should be known where a given syndrome or disease is being listed.

Even the availability of glossaries, however, cannot ensure an operational definition of a diagnostic term. To attain this desideratum, we must specify more clearly the way in which the information regarding a given person should be collected and the way the data obtained are to be integrated. Systematic structured interviews with predesigned item choices for recording have given an added reliability to the information collected, and computer programs either based on decision-tree procedures or utilizing Bayesian (17) approaches can provide better uniform integration of the data for diagnostic purposes. But these diagnoses, despite their high reliability and reproducibility, are no better than the clinician who developed the decision tree. Only continued follow-up studies relating the diagnosis to outcome of specific treatment, to duration of illness, to eventual outcome, and so forth, can provide us with the validity criteria for the diagnosis, even though we have the highest degree of reliability.

Why is it that, despite the available techniques, it is still very difficult to diagnose schizophrenia accurately? One reason for the difficulty is the confusion between the *disorder* present in the patient and the *illness* which he exhibits. Adolf Meyer hinted at this necessary differentiation, but his suggestion was rarely implemented. If we define a disorder as the focal process and the corresponding illness as the combined effect of the focal process and the response of the patient to it, including the patient's response to society's attitudes, it becomes clear why the picture presented by schizophrenia is so heterogeneous and the variety of treatments so diverse. Until we can separate the focal disorder from its effect on the premorbid personality, i.e., the total picture presented by the illness, we shall be caught in an undecipherable puzzle.

Because of the great difficulty in defining schizophrenia, several prominent clinicians have begun to doubt whether schizophrenia really exists, or, if it does exist, whether, in fact, it is merely a life-style rather than a disorder. Rather than get into that thicket, however, I suggest that we recognize that all natural phenomena are approached from two aspects: facts and fictions. Facts deal with the ostensible nature of objects and events—things you can point your finger at. Fictions are categories we use to hold facts together. Of facts, we ask if they are true. Of fictions, we ask only if they are useful. They remain useful only insofar as they serve some good purpose, such as the selection of therapy, prediction of outcome, etc. For this reason, the question of whether schizophrenia is a myth must be altered to whether schizophrenia is a useful concept.

And what evidence do we have that the concept of schizophrenia is useful?

It has been claimed for some time that schizophrenia does

not observe cultural boundaries and is evenly distributed in all cultures—in other words, that schizophrenia is not merely the product of Western culture, but that it exists universally in all cultures and is an indigenous human condition. The recent WHO International Pilot Study of Schizophrenia (18) has provided direct evidence for this claim in investigating admissions to mental hospitals in nine Field Research Centers in the following countries: Colombia, Czechoslovakia, Denmark, India, Nigeria, Taiwan, the U.S.S.R., the U.K., and the U.S.A. A sufficiently wide spectrum of 1202 patients warranted making crosscultural inferences regarding the presence of schizophrenia.

A systematic structured interview of the type described earlier for the U.S.-U.K. study was administered, using items that differentiated significantly between those patients diagnosed as schizophrenic and those diagnosed in other categories. After some winnowing and sifting, 69 items had been selected and subjected to a discriminant function analysis to pick out the items that had the highest weight in separating the two contrasted groups. Twelve items were selected with the highest weights.

The items found to be indicative of schizophrenia were of three types, as shown in Tables A - D.

Table A gives the items which counterindicated schizophrenia. It will be noted that all of these items deal with disorders of mood and sleeping disturbance most characteristic of affective disorders and in this way ruled out schizophrenia.

Table B shows the items dealing with delusions.

Table C shows the items dealing with disturbance in communications and Table D shows the items dealing with poor insight and restricted affect.

When these 12 items were utilized as a 12-point scale and applied to each of the 1202 patients in the WHO project, it was possible to determine how many of the patients diagnosed as schizophrenic scored high or low on this new diagnostic scale.

TABLE A

ITEMS OF THE PSE UNFAVORABLE TO
A DIAGNOSIS OF SCHIZOPHRENIA

Sign or symptom	PSE Observation or question	r
Waking early	Have you been waking earlier in the morning and remaining awake? (Rate positive if 1 to 3 hours earlier than usual.)	.83
Depressed facies	Facial expression sad, depressed.	.73
Elation	Elated, joyous mood.	.67

Based on Table 2 in Carpenter, W.T.Jr., Strauss, J.S. and Bartko, J.J. "Flexible System for the Diagnosis of Schizophrenia: Report from the WHO International Pilot Study of Schizophrenia." Science, 1973, 182, No. 4118, 1275-1277.

TABLE B

ITEMS OF PSE DEALING WITH
DELUSIONS FAVORING A DIAGNOSIS
OF SCHIZOPHRENIA

Sign or symptom	PSE Observation or question	r
Widespread delusions	How widespread are patient's delusions? How many areas in patient's life are interpreted delusionally?	.74
Bizarre delusions	Are the delusions comprehensible?	.69
Nihilistic delusions	Do you feel that your body is decaying, rotting?	None
	Do you feel that some part of your body is missing, for example, head, brain, or arm?	.70
Thoughts aloud	Do you feel that your thoughts are being broadcast, transmitted, so that everyone knows what you are thinking?	.95

Based on Table 2 in Carpenter, W.T.Jr., Strauss, J.S. and Bartko, J.J. "Flexible System for the Diagnosis of Schizophrenia: Report from the WHO International Pilot Study of Schizophrenia." Science, 1973, 182, No. 4118, 1275-1277.

TABLE C

**ITEMS OF PSE DEALING WITH
DISTURBANCES IN COMMUNICATION
AND INTERPERSONAL RELATIONSHIPS
FAVORING DIAGNOSIS OF SCHIZOPHRENIA**

Sign or symptom	PSE Observation or question	r
Incoherent speech	Free and spontaneous flow of incoherent speech	.74
Poor rapport	Did the interviewer find it possible to establish good rapport with patient during interview?	.86
Unreliable information	Was the information obtained in this interview credible or not?	.73

Based on Table 2 in Carpenter, W.T.Jr., Strauss, J.S. and Bartko, J.J. "Flexible System for the Diagnosis of Schizophrenia: Report from the WHO International Pilot Study of Schizophrenia." Science, 1973, 182, No. 4118, 1275-1277.

TABLE D

**ITEMS OF PSE DEALING WITH
INSIGHT AND AFFECT FAVORING A
DIAGNOSIS OF SCHIZOPHRENIA**

Signs or symptom	PSE Observation or question	r
Poor insight	Overall rating of insight	.85
Restricted affect	Blank expressionless face.	.62
	Very little or no emotion shown when delusion or normal material is discussed which would usually bring out emotion.	.63

Based on Table 2 in Carpenter, W.T.Jr., Strauss, J.S. and Bartko, J.J. "Flexible System for the Diagnosis of Schizophrenia: Report from the WHO International Pilot Study of Schizophrenia." Science, 1973, 182, No. 4118, 1275-1277.

TABLE E

**PERCENT OF 1202 PATIENTS DIAGNOSED
AS SCHIZOPHRENIC OR NONSCHIZOPHRENIC
ACCORDING TO NUMBER OF CRITICAL
ITEMS WHICH THEY SHOWED ON INTERVIEW**

	Diagnosis		
	Schizophrenic		Nonschizophrenic
No. of critical items	Percent attaining critical score	Percent failing to attain critical score	Percent attaining critical score
4 or more	91	9	33
5 or more	80	20	17
6 or more	65	35	5
7 or more	41	59	1
8 or more	21	79	0

Based on Table 3 in Carpenter, W.T.Jr., Strauss. J.S. and Bartko, J.J. "Flexible System for the Diagnosis of Schizophrenia: Report from the WHO International Pilot Study of Schizophrenia." Science, 1973, 182, No. 4118, 1275-1277.

Table E shows the proportion of schizophrenics and of non-schizophrenics who could be classified correctly or incorrectly (false positives and false negatives) depending on the breaking point chosen of the 12-point scale.

Thus, if the breaking point is taken as 4, 91% of the schizophrenics are classified correctly and 9% are false negatives, but 33% of the non-schizophrenics would also be classified as schizophrenic, which is too high a proportion of false positives to be acceptable. However, if we take a score of 8 as our breaking point, 21% of the schizophrenics are correctly classified and not a single non-schizophrenic is misclassified—no false positives. This is accomplished at some sacrifice since 79% of schizophrenics fail to attain a sufficiently high score to belong, but the sacrifice may be worthwhile since, though we fail to include all schizophrenics, we succeed in eliminating the non-schizophrenic, thus producing a "core group."

Even though not all individuals labeled schizophrenic belong to the core group, no non-schizophrenic belongs to it, and, therefore, if one desires to select a group of schizophrenics about whom there would be a consensus, these 12 items can serve as a basis for selection.

If one is willing to run the risk of including a small proportion of false positives, he could select a group having only 6 or more critical items in common, and this would include about two-thirds of the total schizophrenic group and only 5% of the non-schizophrenics.*

Thus, it can be concluded that it is possible to identify a core group of schizophrenic patients which has a distinctive pattern of symptoms and that there are patients belonging to this group in every Center in the study.

Finally, the genetic evidence for the existence of a strain of schizophrenia is unmistakeable. While the newly proposed hypothesis by Rosenthal, Wender, and Kety (19) for the inheritance of a schizophrenic spectrum rather than of a specific schizophrenic disorder is somewhat baffling, it nevertheless speaks for the usefulness of the *concept* of schizophrenia, if not for the existence of the condition itself. As Kety has pointed out, if it is a myth, it is an inherited myth!

Thus far we have dealt with the classification of hospitalized mental patients. How well do our diagnostic schemes hold up when we examine a sample of the general population? In other words, how well can we discriminate the well from the ill among those who do not come for help?

If we are to be fair to ourselves and to our colleagues, as well as to the public who put their trust in us, we must admit that we are not as successful in determining whether a given person who has *not* come for help belongs in a diagnostic category as we are in those who have come for help. Apparently, then, un-

---

* This study contained a self-replication, but the table gives the average results for the original sample and the replicated sample.

less an individual in need of treatment assumes a patient role, he will be difficult to detect as mentally ill and, of course, will be difficult to treat. As a matter of fact, mere assumption of a patient role by simulating psychopathology will often bring about admission to a mental hospital, as Rosenhan (20) has recently demonstrated.

But even if we were more successful in descriptive psychopathology, we could not rest, since descriptive diagnosis never cured anyone. We must look for causes if we hope to advance.

A second admission we must make is that as far as etiology or cause is concerned, we are abysmally ignorant. We have had some successes in unraveling the causes of such disorders as general paresis, pellagra with psychosis, and some of the mentally retarded states, but even these victories have been pyrrhic, since the moment the cause of a disorder becomes known, it is lost to psychopathology. Other disciplines take over our hard-won victories and we are left with the disorders of unknown origin.

What does one do when faced with abysmal ignorance? All we can do is resort to the fiction referred to earlier and imagine "as if" causes. But these fictions are not the end of our search; they are only a beginning. The scientific fictions we invent, the scientific models we construct, give rise to certain expectancies —to certain hypotheses, if you will—and these can be tested for their tenability. Thus, the fictions do not remain fixed dogmas but are flexible structures which bend to the weight of the data produced in testing their tenability.

For this reason, good models die young and from their ashes rise, phoenix-like, their successors. Only untestable models remain monolithically fixed in absoluteness.

What are the models that have been proposed in addition to the popular medical model? I suggest the following types (20a):

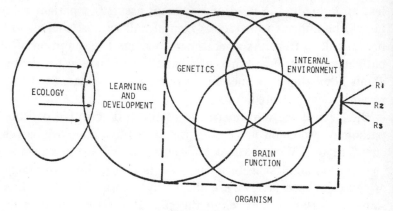

FIGURE 3
Scientific Models of Etiology.

There are, on the one hand, models representing the field theory approach and, on the other hand, those which represent the molecular or medical approach within the dotted square. The field theory approach begins with the ecological model which, simply stated, assumes that man's development in health as well as illness depends on the ecological niche he occupies, as measured by its physical, social, cultural, economic, and educational parameters.

At the opposite pole is the genetic model, which assumes that health and illness are predicated on the genetic equipment man is born with. The middle ground between these two positions is held by the developmental and learning theory models, which lean towards field theory, and the internal environment and neurophysiological (brain function) models, which lean towards the molecular.

The developmental model focuses on the transitional phases between the stages of man's development—from fertilized ovum, to foetus to neonate, childhood, adolescence, adulthood, middle age, and the senium—as the danger points at which development may go awry. The learning theory model is, simply, that man learns to become sick according to the same behavioral laws which govern his normal development. The internal environment model stipulates that the roots of man's illnesses are to be sought in his metabolism, body fluids, and body chemistry in general. The neurophysiological model concentrates on the functioning of man's nervous system and its capacity to take in and process information.

The evidence produced by these various models for causation of mental disorders would require a great deal of space, but I will try to provide a brief summary here.

Ecological Model

The evidence for the ecological model is based on studies of the relation of socioeconomic status to schizophrenia which Faris and Dunham (21) began in the '30s, and which have raised the troubling question of what is cause and what is effect. Does low economic status breed schizophrenia or does schizophrenia gravitate to low economic status? An exciting research design has been proposed by the Dohrenwends (22) to answer this question. But for the time being, the only evidence available for a causal link between sociocultural factors and schizophrenia is the work of H. B. M. Murphy (23) in his examination of data on admission rates for schizophrenia in a variety of ethnic groups composed of both Catholic and non-Catholic subgroups. Across all of the ethnic groups he studied, the Catholic subgroups invariably had the higher admission rates for schizophrenia in males. He tries a variety of possible explanations, among which are the abstemious asexual model for Catholic youth provided by the priest and the nun. Another possibility is that the males in Catholic families do not receive adequate preparation for competing in the outside world. It is possible, however, that the Catholic subgroups may utilize hospital facilities more than the non-Catholic, and this may explain the observed difference.*

A rather striking example of social causation, or social labeling, is afforded by Ackerknecht (24) in his reference to reports that among some South American Indians a very disfiguring spirochaetal infection of the skin, known as pinto, is so widespread that almost all men suffer from it. The few who escape infection are regarded as ill and are precluded from marriage. If we were to liken the stressful pressures of the Puritan ethic for getting jobs and making a living as an infectious agent in our culture, we might emerge with the probability that the small percentage of our population who are not infected by the Puritan ethic might be regarded in some quarters as sick and often be prevented from marrying. This could in fact be the basis for labeling some individuals as schizophrenic.

Developmental Model

Perhaps one of the most vocal proponents of the developmental model is last year's Dean Award winner, Dr. Theodore Lidz. Dr. Lidz's (25) elegant classification of families into the schismatic and the skewed marks an advance in the taxonomy of family types and a most plausible basis for the development of schizophrenia. One can only marvel at the careful painstaking methods he has developed. Without controls, however, it is difficult to fathom whether Dr. Lidz is not actually providing us with a taxonomy of so-called normal family life. Whether his analysis will prove of value to schizophrenics and their families is a hopeful but yet-to-be-realized ambition.

Lidz's concept of decentering, in which the child frees himself from parental dominance in favor of peer group relationships, lends itself to examination experimentally. As a matter of fact,

---

* This is found not to be the case for admissions for depression, but whether it holds true for schizophrenia is not yet known.

one of our former students, Dr. Dolores Kreisman (26), under our guidance, studied the development of adolescent friendship patterns during the preschizophrenic period and contrasted this with development in normals. The outcome indicated that while by and large there was no great difference in the number of friends, intensity of friendship, etc., there was one remarkable difference. The measure of intimacy differentiated the two groups significantly, the normals having the higher scores.

One of the principles prominent in developmental theory is the principle of critical periods—that certain events are crucial for the occurrence of certain types of developments if they occur at a critical juncture. Coming too early, they are ineffective; too late, the particular developmental progress is irretrievably lost. Thus, separation of neonate from mother may not be as crucial at age 6 days as at age 6 months. Similarly, being orphaned at age 5 is more critical than at age 15.

One of the most striking proofs offered for the role of family interaction in the development of schizophrenia comes from Bateson, Jackson, and Haley (27) in their double-bind hypothesis. Here, too, unfortunately, while it is a very persuasive hypothesis, it fails to differentiate normal from abnormal families. Recent investigations have found normal families to be characterized by similar double-bind patterns.

Some of the most negative results on the question of family interaction as a force in the production of schizophrenia in the offspring come from an unexpected quarter, Manfred Bleuler, who has long had an interest in the importance of the family of schizophrenics, an area of interest first promulgated by his fellow countryman, Adolf Meyer. Bleuler's recent book (28), reviewed by Sir Aubrey Lewis (29), focuses on the interplay between patients' lives and those of their nearest relatives in the follow-up of 208 probands.

He found that from 5% to 7% of the parents of the schizophrenic probands were themselves schizophrenic, with mothers affected twice as frequently as fathers. Thus, the vast majority of schizophrenics are raised by presumably normal parents.

Only 25% of the probands showed schizoid features premorbidly, with 18% schizoid in school. Only 14% came from homes in which conditions were appalling. Premorbid occupational levels were similar to that of the parents (fathers) and no different from the distribution in the general population, confirming an earlier study in England by Goldberg and Morrison (30). Unhappy conditions in childhood (broken homes and the like) were not related to deteriorating course in schizophrenia.

Death of parents seemed to have a salutary effect on 7 patients with a pronounced ambivalence towards their parents. Only 9% of the siblings of the probands were found to be schizophrenic.

Eighty-four percent of the married children of the probands were married happily even though they had been raised by schizophrenic parents. Three of the schizophrenic parents had schizophrenic spouses to whom a total of 5 children were born. Despite the double hazard of noxious heredity and family upbringing, 3 of the 5 were mentally healthy.

Bleuler's findings would indicate that the effect of deviant family upbringing seems to be not as noxious as the literature claims.*

Learning Model

Several hypotheses have been proposed for the etiology of schizophrenic behavior based on learning principles. Among these are (a) superstitious behavior, (b) effects of intermittent reinforcement, and (c) conditioned reinforcement. In addition, Salzinger (31) of our unit has provided the immediacy hypothesis as an underlying explanation of schizophrenic behavior.

---

* A condensation of Chapter F of Manfred Bleuler's 1972 book appears in "The Offspring of Schizophrenics" in the *Schizophrenia Bulletin*, NIMH Issue No. 8, Spring 1974, pp. 93-108.

1.   Superstitious behavior

This type of behavior occurs in situations where responses are "conditioned by reinforcers that are actually occurring at random (32)." Since temporal contiguity between response and reinforcer is all that is needed to establish conditioning, the subject cannot tell the difference between a reinforcer that the experimenter delivers and a reinforcer that happens to be contiguous to his response by sheer chance. Thus, it is quite clear why animals as well as humans will learn to do things for which there is no systematic "real reinforcement contingency." Is it not possible that in a society as complex as ours, with all of its recurring stimuli, such chance stimuli might inadvertently and unnoticeably acquire control over some people's behavior? Is this the basis for ritualistic behavior? Compulsive behavior?

2.   Intermittent reinforcement

That even aperiodic non-systematic and non-continuous or inconsistent reinforcements may nevertheless condition behavior is an important factor in the utilization of learning theory in explaining abnormal behavior and its maintenance. The intermittent reinforcement literature tells us that the inconsistent reinforcing behavior by the mother and/or father most likely serves very strongly indeed, for all its inconsistency, in producing persistent abnormal behavior in the child. The fact that the mother tries very hard not to give in to the child's temper tantrum, but gives in some of the time, is of course the very paradigm which maintains the behavior she is trying to eliminate. The fact that conditioning is more rapid than extinction also makes the intermittent schedule a good candidate for the production of abnormal behavior.

3. Conditioned reinforcement

Events associated with primary reinforcers can themselves become reinforcers. The conditioned reinforcer may also help to explain such seemingly bizarre behavior as the collection of magazines or rags or other apparently worthless objects by patients. That such collecting behavior can be practically eliminated by procedures Ayllon (33) calls "satiation" may simply demonstrate a way of reducing the effectiveness of a conditioned reinforcer (rags or magazines) by presenting it frequently in the total absence of any other reinforcers (primary or conditioned).

A variety of learning theory models are described in a recent book by Salzinger (31), head of our Section on Behavior Analysis and Modification. Among these theories are those of Mednick and of Rodnick and Garmezy, all holders of the Dean Award in former years. I will not detail them at length, but will briefly describe Salzinger's Immediacy Hypothesis as an explanation of schizophrenic behavior. You will note that unlike the other models which have tried to explain schizophrenia as due to some underlying disorder, learning theory models do not postulate an underlying disorder, but regard the specific behavior of the schizophrenic as *"das Ding an sich"*—the disorder itself —and try to indicate how it is maintained and why it continues to occur, regardless of how it may have arisen.

The primary source of schizophrenia, according to Salzinger's approach, is some dysfunction in stimulus control—the schizophrenic's response to stimuli in both the external and internal environment. Unlike normals who view the environment broadly, including both proximate and distant objects and events in time and space, the schizophrenic, according to Salzinger, is bound to respond to immediate stimuli in time and space, and this confinement to immediate stimuli in his responses, interacting with the laws of learning, is sufficient to explain schizophrenic behavior. Since immediately close stimuli are not always the most relevant, the schizophrenic, because of his attraction to immediate stimuli, will appear to respond irrelevantly. This may also explain why the schizophrenic will be more likely to expose himself to stimuli which normals consider aversive, particularly the conditioned aversive (social) ones, since these stimuli would be aversive to him only if he responded to them in terms of their remote conditioning history—something he fails to do. Primary aversive stimuli will, however, be avoided, as is the case with normals, only more so for the schizophrenic, since the primary attributes of the aversive stimuli cannot be adapted to by conditioning as readily as is the case with normals:

> The hypothesis explains schizophrenics' deficit in object constancy by calling attention to the fact that the retinal image is more immediate as a stimulus than the history of the object being viewed. Although the theory states nothing specifically about slower reaction time in schizophrenics than in normals, it follows that a person whose behavior is controlled by immediate stimuli might show a slower response to a given stimulus if other stimuli are present to capture his attention. In the case of no special reinforcement contingency, the immediate stimuli are irrelevant and produce the typical schizophrenic longer reaction time; when there is a reinforcement contingency, then the immediate stimuli reinforce the shorter reactions times. . . . (p. 140). (31)

Genetic Model

The genetic model was in the doldrums for a while because some of its exaggerated claims based on twin studies were deflated during the '60s, but it has received a surge of new interest as a result of the investigation of high risk populations begun by one of the former Dean Award winners, Mednick (34), and because of studies of adoptees by Kety, Rosenthal, et al., also former winners of the Dean Award.*

One of the striking findings of the adoptees studies points to the possibility that, far from being a definitive disorder, schizophrenia covers a wide spectrum of disorders from the very mild to the very severe, and this raises the question of the best method for regarding the schizophrenic process. Should it be a typological approach in which definite subcategories are delineated and regarded as based upon different etiologies, or should it be a dimensional approach in which there is a quantitative continuum between all the various types of schizophrenia even though they may require different types of treatment in conformity with their severity? There is no definitive, final answer at this time.

A problem arises from the general tendency of recent genetic findings to discover spectra of schizophrenic-like behavior, rather than only core schizophrenia, in offspring of schizophrenics and their relatives. Since the genotypic schizophrenic may vary in the expression of his schizophrenia, it is possible that many of the members of our control group may be the bearers of genotypic but unexpressed schizophrenia. Furthermore, if the underlying biochemical substance occurs in genotypic schizophrenia, regardless of whether it affects behavior, the comparison of schizophrenic and normal controls may be nullified since the normal controls could contain an unspecified proportion of unexpressed genotypes of schizophrenia. Thus, many of our negative findings in the biochemical and neurophysiological areas may be suspect. Negative behavioral findings may suffer from the same difficulty. One of the problems facing biochemical

---

* A survey of this field appears in "Children at Risk: The Search for the Antecedents of Schizophrenia. Part 1. Conceptual Models and Research Methods," by Garmezy, N. with the collaboration of Sandra Streitman in *Schizophrenia Bulletin*, NIMH Issue No. 8, Spring 1974, pp. 14-90.

and behavioral investigations today is how to purify the control group by eliminating unexpressed schizophrenic genotypes.

Internal Environmental Model

The internal environmental model has also been in the doldrums until recently because most of the earlier findings seemed to be non-specific to schizophrenia. Beginning with Kety's investigation of cerebral blood flow in schizophrenics in 1948, an important milestone in studies of the internal environment in schizophrenia, the investigations following this etiological model have spread rapidly and widely. Cerebral blood flow did not differentiate schizophrenics as a group and succeeding studies of peripheral metabolic correlates met the same fate. It was not until central synaptic mechanisms became the focus of attention that progress was seen. The advent of drugs which influenced the central nervous system allowed correlation between neurochemical action and clinically observable subjective states. Although many leads turned into blind alleys during the last two decades, as Kety (35) points out in his recent Paul Hoch Award address, two hypotheses emanating from this early work are still very promising and have led Kety to assume a very optimistic stance regarding further progress. The findings I am reporting here are drawn from Kety's paper.

The first is the transmethylation hypothesis, based on which nicotinamide was suggested as a treatment for schizophrenia since it is a methyl acceptor and would be expected to drain away from the abnormal pathways methyl groups which permitted an accumulation of methylated hallucinogenic substances. Although this treatment turned out to be a failure, the transmethylation hypothesis received support from another quarter. When methionone, which favors transmethylation, was administered, it exacerbated psychotic behavior in a significant proportion of schizophrenics, but produced no effect in normals. Despite considerable controversy regarding possible alternative explanations, transmethylation is still a viable hypothesis.

The second hypothesis postulates that the disturbance in central catecholamine synapse may account for the crucial vulnerability of the schizophrenic. Evidence for this comes from the great similarity between the toxic psychosis induced by amphetamine and schizophrenia. Since amphetamine releases dopamine and norepinephrine at catecholamine-containing nerve endings, Snyder and his group (36) attempted to determine which of these two types of nerve endings were involved in amphetamine-produced psychotic and stereotyped behavior in man and animals. They concluded that dopamine rather than norepinephrine receptors were involved.

Further evidence for this hypothesis came from the finding that phenothiazines produced a blockade of dopamine receptors in the brain. Thus, if the psychosis produced by amphetamine is analogous with endogenous psychoses, and if both are in some way related to some malfunction in dopaminergic systems, then one can appreciate that the alteration in dopamine metabolism produced by phenothiazine can ameliorate schizophrenic behavior. It will be fascinating to see how the detailed mechanisms of action of these two different drugs, amphetamines and phenothiazines, will eventually explain this.

Furthermore, if the analogy between amphetamine psychosis and schizophrenia is tenable, phenothiazines are to be regarded not as mere tranquilizers providing only symptomatic relief, but as counteracting neurochemically the schizophrenic process itself.

Following the discovery of genetic markers for manic-depressive psychosis in color blindness and the Hg blood group, Wyatt et al (31) proposed that monoamine oxidase may similarly serve as a genetic marker for schizophrenia. This substance is markedly reduced in the platelets of schizophrenics and is also found in reduced quantity in the non-schizophrenic member of pairs of monozygotic twins discordant for schizophrenia.

While much remains to be done in unraveling the role of the

internal environment in the causation of schizophrenia, the outlook has never been brighter.

Neurophysiological Model

Since the birth of the concept of dementia praecox and its subsequent transformation into schizophrenia, the underlying basis for determining the presence of this disorder has inhered in the contrast between a sound sensorium and an unsound mind, i.e., the presence of thought disorder, ambivalence, loose association, and so forth, in a person whose sensory and perceptual capacities are intact. This dictum has gone unchallenged for almost a century and has dissuaded many experimental psychologists from examining the psychophysiological, sensory, and perceptual functioning of schizophrenics.

More recently, it has become quite clear that the physiological and sensory functioning of the schizophrenic is *not* as free of deviations as had been thought. Crude global tests and techniques have always yielded differences between schizophrenics and normals to the detriment of the former, but such differences could usually be attributed to such global factors as lack of attention, motivation, etc. The more sophisticated and well-controlled the techniques became (e.g., choice reaction time, perceptual constancy, size constancy, etc.) the smaller became the differences, until they finally disappeared when attention was paid to the obvious sources of poorer performance—motivation, attention, difficulty of task, etc.

Recently, however, a group of techniques has emerged which seems to find differences between schizophrenics and non-schizophrenic patients and normals which will not go away under the most exacting controlled conditions. To be sure, the differences are not as dramatic as those found with the more global, uncontrolled techniques, but they are nevertheless real and must be dealt with.

These differences have emerged because of two developments. First, the global diagnosis of schizophrenia and depression and personality disorders, based upon free-floating interview techniques, has been replaced in some laboratories by more objective systematic interviews which support the clinical diagnoses with a dimensional profile revealing the underlying psychopathology that characterizes the patient. And, second, an advance has come from progress in the field of physiological sensory and perceptual techniques which provide brief stimuli that elicit responses within the first 1,000 milliseconds. Such techniques are usually somewhat freer than the older techniques from the influence of motivation, prior learning and experience, etc.—in other words, from cultural adhesions to the task. Among these are certain types of reaction time experiments, temporal energy integration, auditory interaction of successive sound stimuli, and evoked potentials, to cite only a few.

To test whether the schizophrenic processes information through his central nervous system differently than the normal does, without involving the complications that ordinarily beset clinical testing, the task must be very simple. One task that can serve this purpose is simple reaction time, such as lifting the finger when a stimulus appears. Secondly, it should, if possible, be a task in which the schizophrenic "excels" the normal; otherwise, poorer performance could be blamed on lack of motivation. Third, it should reflect sensory or perceptual processes and not attitudinal factors. One source of attitudinal bias is eliminated by using forced-choice methods in which the subject must indicate which one of three stimuli is the odd one, reducing the degree to which differences found between schizophrenics and normal might be a reflection of their willingness to take risks in making a judgment. When the forced-choice method was used, Critical Flicker Fusion (CFF) failed to differentiate schizophrenics from normals, while the other psychophysical methods claimed that schizophrenics had higher thresholds (lower cps). On examining CFF by means of signal detection theory techniques in which sensitivity is separated from attitudinal criteria, it became clear that schizophrenics were not less sensitive, but more cautious; they required a lower rate of alternation of the light before they would be willing to judge the stimulus as flickering (38).

The following techniques from our Psychophysiology laboratories headed by Dr. Samuel Sutton (39) found schizophrenics to differ from, and in some instances even excel, the performances of normals and non-schizophrenic patients.

1. Critical duration

The Bunsen-Roscoe law states that up to a specified critical duration, intensity and time are interchangeable so that a bright stimulus acting for a few milliseconds will produce the same response as a less bright stimulus acting for a longer period, provided the total energy (product of intensity and time) remains constant. When the critical duration is passed, not all the energy of the stimulus is integrated and consequently some of it gets "lost" and does not affect the response. It is as if the cup of energy runs over when the critical duration is past, and the excess energy drains off. Consequently, reaction time which is inversely related to energy remains constant during the critical duration period since the total energy is integrated, but increases when the critical duration is surpassed since now there is less effective energy in the stimulus.

As a result of some preliminary investigations by Sutton (39), it was hypothesized that the critical duration for schizophrenic patients for light pulses was approximately 4-6 mscs, considerably shorter than for non-schizophrenic patients and schizophrenic patients, non-schizophrenic patients, and normals were compared by Collins (40) for their reaction time to a 4 msc pulse of light and a 6 msc pulse of light when both pulses contained the same amount of energy. The 6 msc pulse contained normals. In order to verify this preliminary finding, a group of two pulses of 2 msc each separated by a 2 msc dark period. This dark interval is well below the perceptual threshold so that the two stimuli were perceived as continuous by all the subjects.

The results vindicated Dr. Sutton's preliminary findings. The critical duration for the schizophrenic group was indeed shorter than for the non-schizophrenics and normals. The schizophrenics showed an increase in their reaction time to the 6 msc pulse, while the reaction time of the normals and non-schizophrenics was unchanged. Since 3 of the 10 patients in the schizophrenic group differed from their peers by not showing a significant increase to the 6 msc pulse, an examination of their other characteristics was undertaken. They were quite similar to their schizophrenic peers except for one factor—they showed little or no speech disorganization as measured by a systematic structured interview which was administered to patients and normals alike. In contrast, 6 of the 7 schizophrenics who raised their reaction time to the 6 msc pulse showed high scores on the dimension of speech disorganization, a factor which probably reflects thought disorder. It should be noted that this difference between schizophrenics and others cannot be blamed on lack of motivation or interest on the part of the speech-disordered schizophrenics, for they are, in fact, sensitive to a difference in the stimulus which escapes the normals and their schizophrenic and non-schizophrenic peers. No amount of effort in trying to get normals to sense the difference has succeeded thus far.

After refining our measures of speech disorganization and applying them to a new group of patients, we plan to apply the laboratory technique again to the new group to see how our initial finding holds up, hoping to be able to clarify our classification problem and obtain more homogeneous groups.

2. Reaction time to shift in sensory modality

Ever since Shakow's finding on the effect of duration of foreperiod on reaction time, which he reported in his Dean Award Lecture (34), we have wondered whether the observed effect is due to the difference between schizophrenics and normals in time judgment, an area so well studied by Lhamon and Goldstone (41), or whether it is a reflection of segmental set—the inability of the schizophrenic to maintain a set. Our own work in this area may cast light on this question. Instead of varying foreperiods, we varied stimuli—light and sound—and noted that when similar stimuli follow each other (ipsimodal stimuli) reaction time tends to decrease, but when different stimuli follow each other (crossmodal stimuli), reaction time increases. This effect is much greater in schizophrenics than in normals and the difference between schizophrenics and normals is enhanced when the guess that the subject has made of the identity of the stimulus, before it is presented, turns out to be right rather than wrong.

To explain this phenomenon, we first resorted to Shakow's set hypothesis that the patient may expect one of the stimuli; if the other is presented instead, it may take longer for him to react. To test this, we told the subject beforehand what the next stimulus would be, and verified that he correctly placed his finger on the button representing the modality of the next stimulus. Here there was no uncertainty, and a definite set compatible with the imminent stimulus was established.

Yet a greater retardation due to the modality shift persisted in the reaction time of schizophrenics as compared to normals. Apparently the shift in modality, regardless of the compatibility of the set, produced the retardation.

We then went on to examine Shakow's data more carefully (42) and found that when two identical foreperiods succeed each other, the reaction time to the second is not changed, but when two foreperiods of different duration succeed each other, the reaction time increases. Thus, if we view the foreperiod and the succeeding stimulus as a pattern, we can regard two successive identical foreperiod-stimulus combinations as if they were ipsimodal (ipsitemporal) in nature and two successive non-identical foreperiod-stimulus combinations as crossmodal (heterotemporal), and find longer latency in the latter case.

3. Auditory findings

The long-held claim that the auditory threshold of mental patients is no different from that of normals can no longer be accepted. Bruder, Sutton, Babkoff, Gurland, Yozawitz and Fleiss* have demonstrated that the threshold is higher in manic-depressives and, here again, the use of forced-choice and signal detection theory methods eliminates the possibility that lack of motivation is the cause of the difference.

Addressing a somewhat different question, the authors presented randomly either a click which was 25 decibels (db) above each subject's absolute threshold, followed 15 milliseconds later by a click which was 10 decibels above the subject's absolute threshold, or the more intense 25 decibel click by itself. Subjects were to lift their finger from a key as rapidly as possible on the presentation of either stimulus package.

They found that the average reaction time for normals to the paired clicks, the 25 followed by the 10, was only very slightly faster than the average reaction time to the 25 db click by itself. However, for the manic-depressive patients, there was a much larger improvement in reaction time for the paired clicks than for the single intense click presented by itself. Here, then, we have evidence that the patients were benefiting more from the presence of the 10 db click than were the normals. The manic-depressive patients are in this sense more "sensitive" to the presence of the 10 db click and in that sense performing better.

These manic-depressive patients were part of the U.S. sample in the U.S.-U.K. study (43,13) who were originally diagnosed as schizophrenic by their local state hospital clinicians, but were found to be manic-depressive by the project team. The inclusion of their data in a paper devoted to schizophrenia is indicative of the difficulties produced by inadequate diagnostic procedures. The patients who were diagnosed as schizophrenics by the pro-

---

* "Auditory Signal Detectability and Facilitation of Reaction Time in Psychiatric Patients and Non-Patients." Unpublished manuscript, Biometrics Research Unit.

ject team did not differ from normals in their performance on the auditory tasks.

4. Comparison of evoked potential and reaction time results

When our Unit became disenchanted with the available clinical psychological tests because of their dependence on motivation, attention, and interest, as well as because of their lack of independent contribution to diagnosis and their failure in prognosis as Windle (44) pointed out, we turned our attention to the classic categories of human behavioral responses: physiological, sensory, perceptual, psychomotor, and conceptual, and devised a Mendelejeff-like table for classifying these five types of responses according to the kinds of stimuli that can evoke them (45).

These stimuli could vary from the idling state, when no stimulus was presented, to energy stimuli in which the response reflected the intensity of the stimulus, to signal stimuli in which the response depended more on the acquired or inborn significance or meaning of the stimulus. We tried to devise specific experimental situations in which each type of stimulus would elicit the specified category of response. More recently, we gave up this heterogeneous approach and decided instead to utilize the same type of response but elicit it by the different types of stimuli. We selected the physiological response as the "carrier wave" on which to impose the energy and signal loads and noted the variation produced in the response, selecting the evoked potential as one of our measures. We similarly chose reaction time as another measure of the effect of energy and signal types of stimuli. Our plan was to see whether the patterning of the evoked potential and of the reaction time responses to these stimuli would differentiate schizophrenics from other mentally ill persons and normals.

While it is quite clear that not all the rubrics in our grand design will show differences between the mentally disordered and normals, it is likely that the patterning of the responses across the rubrics may yield interesting differential data. Since each of these processes can be detected in the evoked potential, the effect of various cognitive factors such as uncertainty on the average evoked potential can be noted. We have found that some evoked potential components behave differently in schizophrenics as compared to normals and depressives.

Similarly, we can regard the psychomotor response in reaction time as a measuring device for the various loads imposed on the physiological response since it is a less demanding task than those which some of the other psychophysical tasks impose. It might be interesting to compare the influence of some of the cognitive loads on both the purely physiological response —the evoked potential—and the psychomotor response—reaction time. As will be noted from Figure 4 (46) the different loads seem to influence changes in contrary directions when schizophrenics and normals are compared.

When the state of certainty (knowledge of which stimulus is to be presented is given beforehand) is compared with that of uncertainty (no foreknowledge), the schizophrenic shows the greater change in reaction time, but the normal shows the greater change in average evoked potential. Similarly, having guessed correctly rather than incorrectly affects reaction time more in the schizophrenics, but affects average evoked potential more in the normal. Modality switch (when the stimulus shifts from one modality to the other) also affects reaction time more in the schizophrenic, but affects average evoked potentials more in the normals. Thus, the *average evoked potential* is more sensitive to changes in the *normal* in response to the cognitive load of uncertainty, guessing correctly, or shift in stimulus modality while these same cognitive states seem to produce greater changes in the *reaction time* of the *schizophrenic*. While this may appear as a paradox, empirically speaking, it provides us with an unexpected patterning that helps to differentiate schizophrenics from normals even more than if the changes went in

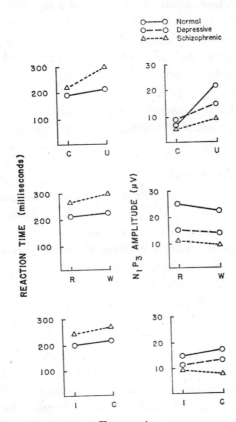

FIGURE 4

Comparison of Reaction Time Data and Evoked Potential Data
on Contrasted Schizophrenics, Depressives, and Normals.

Top panel:	C=certain	U=uncertain
Middle panel:	R=right	W=wrong
Bottom panel:	I=ipsimodal	C=crossmodal

Based on Levit, R.A., Sutton, S., and Zubin, J. Evoked potential correlates of information processing in psychiatric patients. Reprinted from **Psychological Medicine**, 3:487-494, 1973.

the same direction. Perhaps simultaneous recording in the same patient of his reaction time and averaged evoked potential (which we are now doing) will cast even more light on the nature of the observed differential pattern and lead to fractionation of the global heterogeneous schizophrenic group into homogeneous subgroups.

Thus, we have shown that the sensorium of the schizophrenics is not as similar to the sensorium of normals as had been thought.

Therapeutic Intervention

An evaluation of therapeutic intervention requires us to consider whether each of the models we have described dictates the most useful kind of therapy based on the assumed etiology.

The ecological model stipulates that the sources of schizophrenia are to be sought in the ecological niche that the patient occupies in society, and that the causes are the stresses produced by that condition. For example, Cassel (46a) has claimed that the maldistribution of wealth and opportunity and the lack of public health care are causal factors in the high rate of schizophrenia in a rural county of South Carolina.

One of the current approaches to the treatment of schizophrenia based on ecological considerations emanates from the existential-phenomenological view of schizophrenia. Essentially, in its current form it stresses that schizophrenia is a life style and that the best way to treat it is to let it bloom unhampered and even encouraged. By living through his episode, the schizophrenic can gain strength to tide him over the psychotic break and benefit from it as a growth experience. The therapist's function is to be a coequal partner in struggling through the episode rather than a superior dispenser of therapy.

An interesting example of the application of an existential-phenomenological approach is Soteria House (47), modeled to some extent after Laing's (48) Kingsley Hall. One wonders, however, whether there is a way of transferring the modified behavior developed in such places as Soteria House to life outside. Fortunately, Soteria House has provided a systematic description of the kinds of therapeutic endeavors that are applied and a suitable conceived control group, together with a cluster of suitable techniques for measuring the outcome. The results of a current study comparing Soteria patients to those of a community mental health center are being looked to with great anticipation.

The developmental model stipulates that the sources of schizophrenia are to be sought in the transition of man from one stage of development to the next. When the supplies, nutrition, and support required for helping in the transition from one stage to the next are missing or are inadequate, schizophrenia may develop.

What type of therapy is dictated by the developmental model? The recent work in mother-neonate interaction seems to hold out promise for therapeutic intervention. The powerful effect of reinforcement during nursing on the neonate, eye-to-eye contact between mother and child, the possibility of superstitious behavior tendencies arising from the inadvertent reinforcing effect of the nursing act on any or all ongoing behavior, and expectancies which may by chance lead to aggression, submission, dependency, etc., open up new possibilities for investigation. Perhaps these contingencies are so important for subsequent development that we should make them a major focus of our research and clinical efforts.

The learning theory model would lead us to adopt behavior modification methods on the assumption that there is no underlying disorder. Deviant behavior itself, be it phobic depression, psychosomatic, or what not, becomes the target to be eliminated by behavior modification methods.

Certain implications from our models might indeed lead one to engage in the development of behavioral prosthetics for schizophrenia. If we accept Salzinger's immediacy hypothesis, we might develop tape recorders to allow the particular message to be played back in its entirety so that the attention of the schizophrenic would be called to the long-range aspects of the message. In that way he would overcome his fixation on the immediate aspects of his environment. Or perhaps speeding up the message would tend to bring the fullness of the communication into better perspective.

One of the prosthetic devices utilized to improve ward behavior of schizophrenics is a token-economy system in which good performance is immediately rewarded with a token which can be bartered for certain privileges. This system seems to improve ward behavior considerably, often, however, without affecting other aspects of psychopathology or without transfer value to extra-ward behavior. It is not clear what bearing this latter fact has on the validity of the learning theory model. It may be that the therapy treats only peripheral aspects of the total illness picture, or, on the other hand, the therapy may indeed be directed at the core process, but fail to yield permanent results because conditioning techniques are lacking for transferring the effects of behavior modification from the ward into wider social contexts.

The internal environment model would stipulate that somatic and psychopharmacologic methods are the answer. This model has perhaps made the greatest demonstrable advances in the last few decades. The whole armamentarium of psychopharmacology has been turned loose on schizophrenia. While it is generally agreed that we have not yet found the biochemical basis for schizophrenia, we have succeeded in mitigating the condition by the use of drugs. Whether chemotherapy in itself is sufficient or whether it needs the support of psychotherapy or other psychological aids is still not finally answered. May (49) has recently shown, however, that chemotherapy without the aid of psychological intervention seems to do better than psychotherapy without the aid of chemotherapy.

No therapy has as yet been directed at the neurophysiological model, and yet biofeedback experiments may teach us how to control and perhaps abort the neurophysiological substrate of anxiety, depression, and thought disorder.

If we accept Venables's (50) hypothesis that the arousal level of the schizophrenic is different from that of the normal, it may be advisable to train the schizophrenic to lower his arousal level by means of biofeedback. Another possibility is to take the generally slower reaction time of the schizophrenic patient into consideration and deal with him in a way which would compensate for the slowness.

Model for Therapeutic Intervention

In searching for a model for therapeutic intervention, I harked back to the literature on prognosis. This literature is rather vast and varied. I had surveyed it in the early '50s in connection with our prognostic study. The one outstanding effect of this survey was to make us realize that in most cases, long before the disorder struck, the future patient had a personality, a style of life, a degree of adjustment, usually overlooked, which was an important determiner of the change in behavior (illness) which the onset of a disorder produced. No two schizophrenics look alike. In their case, not only are we ignorant of the focus of the disorder, but its interaction with the premorbid personality and the ecological niche so colors the resulting illness that similarities between two schizophrenic patients' behavior may be far less than the differences they exhibit. But premorbid personality and the ecological niche not only determine the illness—the immediate response to the disorder—they also largely determine eventual outcome.

If I were to summarize the results of our prognostic review in one phrase, it would be that the best predictor of outcome is the premorbid personality. In trying to fathom why the premorbid personality plays such an important role in determining outcome, I have proposed the following model for therapeutic intervention.

Let us assume that the schizophrenic is a vulnerable personality who, when subjected to sufficient stress, will be catapulted into an episode. Let us further assume that all episodes are time-limited and that when the episode ends, the patient returns to his premorbid level or close to it. If he had a good premorbid level to begin with, he returns to his premorbid status in society and is regarded as recovered or at least improved. If his premorbid level was poor, what has he got to return to? He could hardly cope before he was catapulted into the episode and he still cannot cope when the episode is ended. As a matter of fact, it is difficult to determine in his case when the episode ends.

We might go a step further, somewhat beyond our data, and assume that all schizophrenics recover from their episodes. What we call chronic schizophrenia would represent a category of individuals who are no longer suffering an episode, but who appear to be still sick because the premorbid personality to which they have returned is not sufficiently well developed to enable them to cope. Furthermore, the hospital stay often teaches them the patient role so well that they develop what Gruenberg (51) has dubbed the SDB—social breakdown syndrome.

The number of such patients is not inconsiderable. Before 1930 and the advent of the shock therapies and the more recent chemotherapies, about one-third of the schizophrenic admissions got out and stayed out, about one-third oscillated back and forth in the hospital, and the remaining third stayed permanently in the hospital (52). Currently, we have continued to release the first third; the middle third, with the help of drugs and other interventions, also generally stays out longer; the last third has become the oscillating group because of its poor premorbid status. It is the last group that needs the special intervention I am discussing here.

One might go still another step further and say, don't bother so much about treating the good premorbids—they'll get well anyhow or will get well quicker with suitable intervention. Concentrate on the poor premorbids and utilize whatever therapeutic talent you have to rehabilitate them, using psychotherapy, behavior modification, chemotherapy, or what not. Of course, a moral issue might arise here. What right have we to remold the personality of the poor premorbid so that he will better fit our social-cultural mold? I suppose our only justification is based on the fact that he came for help. If he does not want to improve his premorbid personality, does not want to adjust to society, well, then he can join Laing's cohorts and remain either unreconstructed or do his thing the best way he knows how, or find an outlet for his latent style with the help of Laingean therapy. Thus, the thrust of intervention is removed from cure to remolding personality—a new venture worthy of our attention.

The variety of approaches presented in this paper has both an advantage and a disadvantage. The advantage inheres in the fact that by pushing each model to its limits, we can uncover more and more of the roots of the disorder. The disadvantage lies in the fact that the interaction between the models is probably of greater importance in understanding the underlying causes than any single model. Thus, genetics alone is necessary but not sufficient, even as noxious ecological niches are necessary to elicit the schizophrenic anlage but not sufficient in themselves to bring it about. The same holds true of all the other models.

Perhaps the best paradigm for viewing the problem is the technique of analysis of variance. In this technique we first examine the main effects, and then, having exhausted this source of variation, we examine the various orders of interaction. This is the most fruitful view to take.

Evaluation of Outcome

Determining criteria for evaluating outcome is one of the most urgent problems we face. It must be realized, however, that there are at least five aspects of evaluation which need consideration. First is the state of well being of the patient based on his own self-assessment; second, the assessment of the therapist; third, the opinion of the family; fourth, the attitude of society as a whole; and fifth, the burden or lack of it which the system of delivery of care has to bear with regard to the former patients. Each of these ways of assessing outcome of illness is biased in the interests of the agent doing the evaluation, and these five ways of assessing outcome are not very highly correlated. The problem, then, becomes one of choosing the best set of weights for combining the five different assessments, or finding an independent measure that will be free of bias.

Several tools have been developed for assessing outcome on the basis of these criteria. The self-evaluation of the patient can be obtained on a set of self-reporting inventories such as the MMPI. The evaluation of the therapist can be obtained by means of a technique developed by Gurland (53, 54) known as the SSIAM, and the systematic structured interview used in diagnosis can be repeated to determine what changes have occurred on follow-up in the psychopathology of the patient. Special measures like the Katz Adjustment Scale (55) can be administered to family members to determine their evaluation of the patient.

The evaluation of the former patient by society, with regard to his reintegration into the social structure, is now being accomplished clinically by sensitive social workers, and attempts at determining his level of coping have been provided by social scientists.

Finally, the degree to which the system of delivery of services gets involved with the patient after his discharge can be measured by outcome indices such as suggested by Burdock (56), in which the proportion of time spent in the hospital after first admission is considered in relation to the ratio of number of discharges to readmissions during the follow-up period. The product of these two factors varies from near zero for the best outcome index to 1.00 for the worst outcome. Those with a zero index enter the hospital for a brief time and never return, while those who achieve an index of 1.00 remain in the hospital continuously.

No one has ever tried to integrate these five measures of outcome into a composite. Perhaps it cannot be done successfully. On the other hand, even if these criteria are not summative, it is possible to utilize typological approaches which would classify individuals into subtypes in accordance with the pattern presented by their status on the five criteria, giving us, once and for all, a systematic structure for assessing outcome.

Summary

What does all this mean? First of all, one can raise the question, as Dubos (57) has done, whether all of our scientific findings have any significance for the human condition—and specifically, have they any significance for the human condition known as schizophrenia?

Thus far we have described the etiological models as blind forces which control man's destiny; to some extent, given the current scene, it is a true picture. For the ecological niche in which man finds himself does determine his well-being, his genetic makeup does limit his potential, his developmental past and learned behavior do confine his future, his internal environment and neurophysiological makeup do control his behavior. And, in fact, we might agree with Dubos that all of these forces are merely the "stage props" for the drama that man is to enact on the stage of life. However, we have left out perhaps the most important determinant of man's stage behavior—his ability to be a self starter, to alter developmental trends, to modify his internal environment as well as his neurophysiological equipment. Unlike other organisms which are shaped by their environment through eons of gradual evolutionary developments, man can shape his own environment if he chooses to do so and has developed the know-how to apply changes not only to the exogenous but also to the endogenous environment. It is in these directions that the future of man's normal development, as well as the containment and improvement of abnormal development, lies. And it need not take eons to accomplish, for we can produce changes for the better even in our own lives and in our own lifetimes (20a).

Meantime, despite the fact that all we now understand and thus are able to control are the mere underpinnings of the stage on which the dramatic action takes place, we still may hope to control the form if not the content of the action. Perhaps the underpinnings of tragedies like schizophrenia are different from the underpinnings of comedies. Perhaps the simple differences which differentiate the schizophrenic—his inability to shift as readily, his shorter critical duration, his lower amplitudes in evoked potentials, and the different patterns produced psychomotorically, as contrasted with perception under the influence of uncertainty, reward, punishment, etc.—constitute the real building blocks of schizophrenia. He begins to feel different and appears to his friends to be different because of the small discrepancies in his behavior. Once these differences become recognized by him and by his peers, the rest of schizophrenia begins to develop. In other words, schizophrenia is "caused" by these small losses of pawns in the game of life—the rest of schizophrenia is merely an epiphenomenon. I realize that this is a highly controversial point of view, but this is what I have come to believe is a possible, though not yet probable, explanation of some types of schizophrenia. In short, schizophrenia occurs in a vulnerable individual when he is subjected to sufficient stressors—and his vulnerability is detectable in the differential patterns of his central nervous system responses. How to manage this vulnerability and protect the individual from succumbing to the disorder are the challenges which this model places before us.

REFERENCES

1. JASPERS, K. *General Psychopathology*. Translated by Hoenig, J. and Hamilton, M. W. Chicago: University of Chicago Press, 1963, p. 667.
2. KRAEPELIN, E. Der psychologische Versuch in der Psychiatrie. *Psychologische Arbeiten*, 1:77, 1896.
3. FREUD, S. *The Standard Edition of the Complete Psychological Works of Sigmund Freud*, Vol. 1. *Project for Scientific Psychology*. London: The Hogarth Press, 1966, pp. 283 ff.
4. VAN GIESON, I., and SIDIS, B. Neuron Energy. *Arch. of Neuropath. and Psychopath.*, 1:1-24, 1898.
5. COTTON, H. The Etiology and Treatment of the So-called Functional Psychoses. *Amer. J. of Psychiat.*, 2:157-210, 1922.
6. KOPELOFF, N., and CHENEY, C. O. Studies in Focal Infection: Its Presence and Elimination in the Functional Psychoses. *Amer. J. of Psychiat.*, 2:139-156, 1922.
7. ZUBIN, J., ERON, L. D., and SCHUMER, F. *Experimental Approaches to Projective Techniques*. John Wiley & Sons, 1965.
8. BURDOCK, E. I. and HARDESTY, A. S. *Structured Clinical Interview*. New York: Springer Publishing Co., 1968.
9. SPITZER, R. L., BURDOCK, E. I. and HARDESTY, A. S. *Mental Status Schedule*. Copyright, 1964.
10. SPITZER, R. L., ENDICOTT, J., FLEISS, J. L. and COHEN, J. The Psychiatric Status Schedule. *Arch. of Gen. Psychiat.*, 23:41-55, 1970.
11. WING, J. K., BIRLEY, J. L. T., COOPER, J. E., GRAHAM, P. and ISAACS, A. D. Reliability of a Procedure for Measuring and Classifying Present Psychiatric State. *British J. of Psychiat.*, 113:499, 1967.
12. KRAMER, M. Some Problems for International Research Suggested by Observations of Differences in First Admission Rates to the Mental Hospitals of England and Wales and of the United States. In *Proceedings of the Third World Congress of Psychiatry*, Vol. 3. Montreal: University of Toronto Press/McGill University Press, 1961, pp. 153-160.
13. COOPER, J. E., KENDELL, R. E., GURLAND, B. J., SARTORIUS, N. and FARKAS, T. Cross-National Study of Diagnosis of the Mental Disorders: Some Results from the First Comparative Investigation. *Amer. J. of Psychiat.*, 125:21-29 (supplement), 1969.
14. GURLAND, B. J., FLEISS, J. L., COOPER, J. E., KENDELL, R. E. and SIMON, R. Cross-National Study of Diagnosis of the Mental Disorders: Some Comparisons of Diagnostic Criteria from the First Investigation. *Amer. J. of Psychiat.*, 125:30-38 (supplement), 1969.
14a. FLEISS, J. L., GURLAND, B. J., and COOPER, J. E. Some Contributions to the Measurement of Psychopathology. *British J. of Psychiat.*, 119:647-656, 1971.

15. HUXLEY, J. S. Introductory: Towards the New Systematics. In *The New Systematics*, J. S. Huxley, ed. Oxford: Clarendon Press, 1940.
16. WORLD HEALTH ORGANIZATION, REGIONAL OFFICE FOR EUROPE. *Published National Statistics on Mental Illness in Europe.* Copenhagen: World Health Organization, 1966.
17. FLEISS, J. L., SPITZER, R. L., COHEN, J. and ENDICOTT, J. Three Computer Diagnosis Methods Compared. *Arch. of Gen. Psychiat.*, 27:643-649, 1972.
18. WORLD HEALTH ORGANIZATION. *Report of the International Pilot Study of Schizophrenia.* Vol. 1. Geneva, 1973.
19. ROSENTHAL, D., WENDER, P. H., KETY, S. S., SCHULSINGER, F., WELNER, J. and OSTERGAARD, L. Schizophrenics' Offspring Reared in Adoptive Homes. In *The Transmission of Schizophrenia*, D. R. Rosenthal and S. S. Kety, eds. Oxford: Pergamon Press, 1968.
20. ROSENHAN, D. L. On Being Sane in Insane Places. *Science*, 179: 250-258, 1973.
20a. ZUBIN, J. Scientific Models for Psychopathology in the '70's. *Seminars in Psychiatry*, 4:283-296, 1972.
21. FARIS, R. E. L. and DUNHAM, H. W. *Mental Disorders in Urban Areas: An Ecological Study of Schizophrenia and Other Psychoses.* Chicago: Chicago University Press, 1939.
22. DOHRENWEND, B. P. and DOHRENWEND, B. S. *Social Status and Psychological Disorder.* New York: Wiley & Sons, 1969.
23. MURPHY, H. B. M. Sociocultural Factors in Schizophrenia: A Compromise Theory. In *Social Psychiatry*, J. Zubin and F. Freyhan, eds. New York: Grune & Stratton, 1968, pp. 74-92.
24. ACKERKNECHT, E. H. *A Short History of Psychiatry.* Translated by S. Wolff. New York: Hafner Publishing Co., 1968, p. 5.
25. LIDZ, T. Family Studies and a Theory of Schizophrenia. Paper presented as the Stanley R. Dean Award Lecture to the American College of Psychiatrists. New Orleans, January 1973.
26. KREISMAN, D. Social Interaction and Intimacy in Preschizophrenic Adolescence. In *The Psychopathology of Adolescence*, J. Zubin and A. M. Freedman, eds. New York: Grune & Stratton, 1970.
27. BATESON, G., JACKSON, D. D., HALEY, J. and WEAKLAND, J. H. Toward a Theory of Schizophrenia. *Behavior Science*, 1:251-264, 1956.
28. BLEULER, M. *Die schizophrenen Geistesstörungen im Lichte langjähriger Kranken-und Familiengeschichten.* (The Schizophrenic Mental Disturbances in the Light of the Long Term Patient and Family Histories). Thieme: Stuttgart, 1972.
29. LEWIS, A. Manfred Bleuler's "The Schizophrenic Mental Disorders," an Exposition and a Review. *Psychological Medicine*, 3:385-392, 1973.
30. GOLDBERG, E. M. and MORRISON, S. L. Schizophrenia and Social Class. *Brit. J. of Psychiat.*, 109:785-802, 1963.

31. SALZINGER, K. *Schizophrenia: Behavioral Aspects.* **New York:** Wiley & Sons, 1973.

32. HERRNSTEIN, R. J. Superstition: A Corollary of the Principles of Operant Conditioning. In *Operant Behavior: Areas of Research and Application.* New York: Appleton-Century-Crofts, 1966.

33. AYLLON, T. Intensive Treatment of Psychotic Behavior by Stimulus Satiation and Food Reinforcement. *Behavior Research and Therapy,* 1:53-61, 1963.

34. DEAN, S. R., ed. *Schizophrenia: The First Ten Dean Award Lectures.* New York: MSS Information Corporation, 1973.

35. KETY, S. S. Progress Toward an Understanding of the Biological Substrates of Schizophrenia. In *Genetics and Psychopathology,* R. R. Fieve, D. Rosenthal and H. Brill, eds. Baltimore: Johns Hopkins, 1974. (In press.)

36. SNYDER, S. H. Catecholamines in the Brain as Mediators of Amphetamine Psychosis. *Arch. of Gen. Psychiat.,* 27:169-179, 1972.

37. WYATT, R. J., MURPHY, D. L., BELMAKER, R., DONNELLY, C., COHEN, S. and POLLIN, W. Reduced Monoamine Oxidase Activity in Platelets: A Possible Genetic Marker for Vulnerability to Schizophrenia. *Science,* 179:916-918, 1973.

38. CLARK, W. C., BROWN, J. C. and RUTSCHMANN, J. Flicker Sensitivity and Response Bias in Psychiatric Patients and Normal Subjects. *J. of Abnormal Psychology,* 72:35-42, 1967.

39. SUTTON, S. Fact and Artifact in the Psychology of Schizophrenia. In *Psychopathology: Contributions from the Biological, Behavioral, and Social Sciences,* M. Hammer, K. Salzinger and S. Sutton, eds. New York: John Wiley, 1973.

40. COLLINS, P. J. Reaction Time Measures of Visual Temporal Integration in Schizophrenic Patients, Other Psychiatric Patients, and Normal Subjects. (Doctoral dissertation, Columbia University.) Ann Arbor, Mich.: University Microfilms, 1972.

41. LHAMON, W. T. and GOLDSTONE, S. Temporal Information Processing in Schizophrenia. *Arch. of Gen. Psychiat.,* 28:44-51, 1973.

42. ZUBIN, J. Problems of Attention in Schizophrenia. In *Experimental Approaches to Psychopathology,* M. L. Kietzman, S. Sutton and J. Zubin, eds. New York: Academic Press, 1974. (In press.)

43. GURLAND, B. J., FLEISS, J. L., COOPER, J. E., SHARPE, L., KENDELL, T. R. and ROBERTS, P. Cross-National Study of Diagnosis of Mental Disorders: Hospital Diagnoses and Hospital Patients in New York and London. *Comprehensive Psychiatry,* 11:18-25, 1970.

44. WINDLE, C. Psychological Tests in Psychopathological Prognosis. *Psychological Bulletin,* 49:452-482, 1952.

45. BURDOCK, E. I., SUTTON, S. and ZUBIN, J. Personality and Psychopathology. *J. of Abnormal and Social Psychiatry,* 56:18-30, 1958.

46. LEVIT, R. A., SUTTON, S. and ZUBIN, J. Evoked Potential Correlates of Information Processing in Psychiatric Patients. *Psychological Medicine*, 3:487-494, 1973.
46a. CASSEL, J. C. Psychiatric Epidemiology. In *American Handbook of Psychiatry*, 2nd ed., Vol. 2, G. Caplan, ed. New York: Basic Books, 1974, pp. 401-410.
47. MOSHER, L. A. Research Design to Evaluate Psychosocial Treatments of Schizophrenia. Proceedings of the IV International Symposium, Turku, Finland, August 4-7, 1971. *Excerpta Medica*, Amsterdam.
48. LAING, R. D. *The Politics of Experience.* New York: Ballantine Books, 1967.
49. MAY, P. R. A. *Treatment of Schizophrenia.* New York: Science House, 1968.
50. VENABLES, P. H. Signals, Noise, Refractoriness, and Storage. Some Concepts of Value to Psychopathology? In *Experimental Approaches to Psychopathology*, M. L. Kietzman, S. Sutton and J. Zubin, eds. New York: Academic Press, 1974. (In press.)
51. GRUENBERG, E. The Social Breakdown Syndrome—Some Origins. *Amer. J. of Psychiat.*, 123:1481-1489, 1967.
52. STAUDT, V. and ZUBIN, J. A Biometric Evaluation of the Somatotherapies in Schizophrenia. *Psychological Bulletin*, 54:171-196, 1957.
53. GURLAND, B. J., YORKSTON, N. J., STONE, A. R., FRANK, J. D. and FLEISS, J. L. The Structured and Scaled Interview to Assess Maladjustment (SSIAM) I: Description, Rationale and Development. *Arch. of Gen. Psychiat.*, 27:259-263 (a), 1972.
54. GURLAND, B. J., YORKSTON, N. J., GOLDBERG, K., FLEISS, J. L., SLOANE, R. B. and CRISTOL, A. H. The Structured and Scaled Interview to Assess Maladjustment (SSIAM): II. Factor Analysis, Reliability, and Validity. *Arch. of Gen. Psychiat.*, 27:264-267(b), 1972.
55. KATZ, M. M. and LYERLY, S. B. Methods for Measuring Adjustment and Social Behavior in the Community: I. Rationale, Description, Discriminative Validity, and Scale Development. *Psychological Reports*, Monograph Supplement 4-V13, 1963.
56. BURDOCK, E. I. and HARDESTY, A. S. An Outcome Index for Mental Hospital Patients. *J. of Abnormal and Social Psychology*, 63:666-670, 1961.
57. DUBOS, R. *American Scholar*, 41:16, 1971.